EARLY HISTORY

OF THE

CHEROKEES

Embracing

Aboriginal Customs, Religion,

Laws, Folk Lore, and

Civilization.

ILLUSTRATED

BY

EMMET STARR

(Copyright 1917 by Emmet Starr.)

Transcribed by

Jeff Bowen

CLEARFIELD

Printed for Clearfield Company by
Genealogical Publishing Company
Baltimore, Maryland
2011

ISBN 978-0-8063-5536-8

Made in the United States of America

Cover photo of Emmet Starr
Courtesy of Victoria Sheffler, Archivist
University Archives, John Vaughan Library
Northeastern State University
Tahlequah, Oklahoma

This volume is respectfully dedicated to my friend,

JOSEPH B. THOBURN,

a man to whom the state owes a dept of gratitude
for his honest, careful and indefatigable research
into the elemental history of Oklahoma.

EMMET STARR.

Sequoyah and fac-simile of his signature. Cherokee genealogy No. V—1[1].

PREFACE.

The purpose of this volume is to present many of the phases of Cherokee Indian history that might not otherwise be preserved and understood.

I am a Cherokee, born in Going Snake District, Cherokee Nation, Indian Territory, on December 12, 1870. I was reared in the Cherokee Nation, received my education in the Cherokee public schools and graduated from the Cherokee National Male Seminary in 1888.

All four of my grandparents were "Old Settler" Cherokees, having settled in the Cherokee Nation "West" prior to 1832.

My father, who had been a soldier in the Confederate Cherokee service, was after I can remember successively deputy sheriff, deputy clerk and judge of Cooweescoowee District, which comprised about one-third of the Cherokee Nation. My father's home (which was three miles from the District court house) and hospitality was open to his friends and in this way I was afforded at an early age the opportunity of listening to the conversations and reminiscences of many of the most brilliant minds among my own people. I listened as a boy to the Adairs, Bells, Rosses, Mayeses and many others who were born reconteurs and savants.

I commenced the collection of material for genealogical and historical work on my people in 1891.

As a result of my work along these lines I am attempting to present to you in this volume a true and correct history of the Cherokees up to the year 1830.

I am using quite a number of photographs of Cherokees, many of whom are living. I have invariably used such pictures as I cared to, using them for type illustrations, and I have not asked permission in any one single instance for the right to use these photographs.

Most of the chief's and assistant chief's pictures are reproduced with permission from the copyrighted originals by Mr. Osborn, the photographer, of Tahlequah.

On account of the fact that the Cherokee tribe became divided into three groups early in the nineteenth century and then later coalesced, it is impossible to write a sequent chronological account of the tribe during this period.

I expect to publish other volumes on the history of the Cherokees.

Respectfully,
EMMET STARR

Claremore, Okla.

Introduction

This Emmet Starr book, *Early History of the Cherokees*, was copyrighted in 1917. It has been meticulously reconstructed as closely as possible to the original through transcription and the scanning of images. Where possible, the images, while not being altered or changed, have been enhanced in order to improve their quality. There are several words and places that were spelled differently throughout the book, but it was felt there was no need to make a notation in order to preserve the integrity of the book because it may be that in 1917 the author and his contemporaries may well have spelled these words differently and found them to be correct during their era. This book was published four years prior to his *History of the Cherokee Indians and Their Legends and Folk Lore*.

This earlier volume appears to be a more complete explanation of some of the origins and customs of the early Cherokees (*e.g.* clans, religion, marriage, laws, and government, to name a few). The later volume contains more genealogical and biographical subject matter.

The original manuscript had a header on the left side with the book's partial title, the header on the right side gave a category and remained constant until the subject changed. This author has created an image index, a subject index which replaces the right-side page headers, and a name index in the back of the book.

There is no doubt that this piece of Native history will be well suited for every library, student, or Cherokee genealogist ever to have touched the volume *History of the Cherokee Indians* as a companion to Mr. Starr's brilliant efforts and dedication to the Cherokee families he worked so hard to preserve.

Jeff Bowen
Gallipolis, OH
NativeStudy.com

EARLY HISTORY OF CHEROKEES.

ABORIGINAL CHEROKEES.

A Distinctive Name.

The name Cherokee has its origin in the Cherokee words; a-che-la, meaning fire, and ah-gi, he takes. The expression has it emination in the belief that at the creation, the Great Spirit gave to this tribe a sacred fire, with the admonition that they were to keep it perpetually burning, and that on this fire the ku-ta-ni or priests were to offer sacrifices.

Ku-ta-ni.

According to the legends, the ancient Cherokees had one family from whom only could the priesthood, or ku-ta-ni, be recruited.

Perfidity of the Ku-ta-ni.

As long as the sacred fire remained common property the success and prosperity of the Cherokees was illimitable, but some designing priests, who watched over it, surreptitiously transferred it to clear white stones, and ever afterwards it could only be seen flashing and flaring in the conical icacati of the adoniska, or conjuror, as he, in its flames claimed to see the image of the present or the portent of the future.

Execution of the Ku-ta-ni.

On account of this crime, every priest and neophyte was executed, thus closing to the Cherokees practically all knowledge of their primal religious practices, as they had been handed down verbally to the elect succession.

Adoniska.

Until the coming of the Christian religion the functions of the ku-ta-ni was essayed in a minimized way by the adoniska, or conjuror, although they held their sway more through the awe with which they impressed the laity than otherwise, as they seldom attained reverence, although some of those of a kindly philosophic nature became greatly beloved.

Clans.

From time immemorial the Cherokee tribe has been divided into seven "peoples" or "families." Tradition says that long ago they dwelt in six separate towns or settlements, each of which was named on account of some distinctive difference it bore from its congenors.

Wolf Town and Deer Town.

At one town it was the custom to catch and pet young wolves; at another, fawns were domesticated. For these reasons the first was called Wolf Town and the second Deer Town.

Bird Town.

A third town was located in a timbered section that was frequented by the nuthatch (possibly sitta pusilla). The Cherokees called this bird the "stealer bird," from its habit of pecking into decayed trees and appropriating the winter supplies of squirrels, rats and other rodents. From these birds the settlement became known as Bird Town, and was often called "Stealer Town;" but this only had reference to the bird after which the town was named and was never said to reflect on the probity of the citizens of this community.

Long Hair Town and Paint Town.

In one town the men wore their hair long, and in another the warriors were always painted and ready for war, being veritable prototypes of the more modern Chicamaugas.[†] They were, respectively, Long Hair Town and Paint Town.

Blind Swamp Town.

A sixth community was separated from the others by a sedgy swamp, in which the vegetation was so dense that a person in passing through it could only see a short distance. On account of this peculiarity

---

[†] See Chicamaugas. Handbook of American Indians.

it was called Blind Savannah or Blind Swamp Town.

Sgatooga.

The Cherokees use the comprehensive term, sgatooga (skiatook), meaning either hamlet, town, neighborhood, state or county, but in this instance the so-called towns were really communities or neighborhoods.

Clans.

The inhabitants of each separate sgatooga were originally designated by their community name, as follows: Wolf Town people, Deer Town people, Bird Town people, Long Hair Town people, Paint Town people and Blind Savannah Town people.

A Democracy.

The members of these towns had equal rights and privileges, as the Cherokee Nation, was always a pure democracy, except during the short lived empire[‡] of Priber (1736-1745).

Maternal Descent.

The "people" was always inherited from the mother (paternal half-brothers and half-sisters, where the mothers were of different clans, were not counted as relatives). Thus if any one of the maternal line of ancestry was a member of another tribe, then the descendants lost their "people" or clan. All members of a "people" or clan were considered to be brothers and sisters, although in most instances they were not of traceable consanguineous relationship.

Older members of the father's "people" were often addressed as father or mother, but this implied relationship was only complimentary; bestowed in cases of friendship, and had no social significance. The closest degree of relationship and filial affection always existed among the members of the same "people," and though the individuals might be strangers to each other, there was always the most sincere fraternal conduct and solicitude practiced between them. No English speaking

---

[‡] See Pickett's Alabama, pages 271 to 277.

family ever preserved a more marked degree of love and respect for all the members of their immediate family than did these "town people" for each other.

Among the ancient Cherokees, if a stranger was traveling through the country and came to a habitation, he, immediately after the salutation of "osao" (all well, or is all well with you?), was asked, "To what 'people' do you belong?" If he belonged to the same "people" as did the householder or his wife, the hospitality was open, the stranger was transformed into a brother and sat by a hearth that was his home in every respect, and he might stay all night, a week, a moon or the rest of his life if he so wished. If the stranger answered that he belonged to another "people" than that of either of the householders, he was directed so that he could find his nearest "town brother" or "sister," with the impression that he would want to see them (although they might be strangers), and did not mean that he was not a welcome guest of the parties with whom he was speaking.

By their customs, the immutable penalty of death, by their own "town people" was imposed on both the man and woman if they married members of their own "town people," and neither position nor condition excused them from the immediate penalty.[§]

Holly People.

You will notice that I have heretofore given the names of six "towns people." I will now relate the facts of the genesis of the "Holly people." Long after the other "peoples" had become separately known, and their customs had become firmly established, a war party of Cherokees found a girl baby lying under a holly busy. They did not know what tribe she belonged to. They took her back to the Cherokee Nation, where she was adopted by a family. She grew to womanhood, married and became the mother of a large family. In order that her descent in the female line could be classified, it was necessary to create another "people," and this was done by bestowing upon them the name of "Holly people," and they were often referred to as the "young people," on account of the name having been established later than the others.

[§] The customs of the several tribes were so dissimilar that it is impossible to give a composite mythological or sociological account of any two of them.

EARLY HISTORY OF CHEROKEES.

Most of the early settlers and traders among the Cherokees were Scotch or English, and seeing a seeming analogy between the Scottish clans and these Indian "peoples," they termed them Wolf clan, Deer clan, Bird clan, Long Hair clan, Paint clan, Blind Savannah clan and Holly clan. Of these, the Wolf clan was the most powerful in number.

"Indian Countrymen."

As the type of the pioneer Scotch and English traders that settled in the several Indian nations of the southeastern portion of the United States were very similar, I append the following account from the preface of "The History of Alabama," published in 1851, by Albert J. Pickett: "In my intercourse with them (the Creek Indians) I was thrown into the company of many old White men, called 'Indian countrymen,' who had for years conducted a commerce with them. Some of these men had come to the Creek Nation before the Revolutionary war and others, being Tories, had fled to it during the war, and after it, to escape from Whig persecution. They were unquestionably the shrewdest and most interesting men with whom I ever conversed. Generally of Scotch descent, many of them were men of some education. All of them were married to Indian wives, and some of them had intelligent and handsome children. From these Indian countrymen I learned much concerning the manners and customs of the Creeks, with whom they had long been associated, and more particularly with regard to the commerce which they carried on with them."

Overhills and Underhills.

Another subdivision of the Cherokee tribe was based on idiom and habitat, and had no essential social or political significance, although almost all writers erroneously ascribe a divisional political status for them. The Overhills lived in the uplands and subsisted for the most part by hunting and fishing. Their habitations were light and portable, so that they could be easily moved to another locality when game became scarce. In speaking they used the sound of "r" and several gutturals, which rendered their speech more dissonant than that of the Underhill brothers, whose language was perfectly liquid, an infrequent sound of "m" being the only labial that they employed.

5

The rich alluvial valleys and coves were preferred by the Underhills, as they depended more on the fruits of the fields for their sustenance. They raised bounteous crops, including corn, beans and tobacco, and having these to barter for the simple implements of husbandry that the early settlers brought from the East, a mutual interest engendered an early friendship. The habitations of the Underhills were more stable than those of the less stationary Overhills.

It seems hardly probable that the beautiful liquid accents of the Underhill Cherokees were those of a people who came from the far north, as did the Iroquois.

Cherokee Territory.

When the Spanish, French and English first came among the Cherokees they were living in North Carolina, South Carolina, Tennessee, Georgia and Alabama. "Their whole country was the most beautiful and romantic in the known world. Their springs of delicious water gushed out of every hill and mountainside. Their lovely rivers meandered, now slowly and gently, through the most fertile valleys, and then, with the precipitancy and fleetness of the winds, rushed over cataracts and through mountain gaps. The forests were full of game, the rivers abounded with fish, the vales teemed with their various productions and the mountains with fruit, while the pure atmosphere consummated the happiness of the blest Cherokees."[*]

"The native land of the Cherokee was the most inviting and beautiful section of the United States."[†]

"The Cherokees occupied the valley of the Tennessee River as far west as the Mussel Shoals and the highlands of Carolina, Georgia and Alabama, the most picturesque and salubrious region east of the Mississippi. Their homes are encircled by blue hills rising beyond hills, of which the lofty peaks would kindle with the early light and the overshadowing night envelop the valleys like a mass of clouds. There the rocky cliffs, rising in naked grandeur, defy the lightnings and mock the loudest peals of the thunderstorm; there the gentle slopes are covered with magnolias and flowering forest trees, decorated with roving

---

[*] History of Alabama, page 141. Albert J. Pickett, 1851.
[†] Annals of Tennessee, page 83. J. G. M. Ramsey, 1853.

climbers and ring with the perpetual note of the whip-poor-will; there the wholesome water gushes from the earth in transparent springs; snow white cascades glitter on the hill sides; through the narrow vales which the abundant strawberry crimsons and coppices of rhododendron and flaming azalea adorn."[‡]

Personality.

"The Cherokees were the mountaineers of aboriginal America and, like all other mountaineers, adored their country, held to and defended it with a heroic devotion, a patriotic constancy and an unyielding tenacity, which cannot be too much admired or eulogized."[†]

William Bartram, the botanist, who visited their country in 1776, says: "The Cherokees in their disposition and manners are grave and steady, dignified and circumspect in their deportment; rather slow and reserved in their conversation, yet frank, cheerful and humane; tenacious of the liberties and natural rights of man; secret, deliberate and determined in their councils; honest, just and liberal, and always ready to sacrifice every pleasure and gratification, even their blood and life itself, to defend their territory and maintain their rights."[‡]

Physical Characteristics.

"The males were larger and more robust than any other of our natives, while the women were tall, slender, erect and of delicate frame, with features of perfect symmetry. With cheerful countenance, they moved about with becoming grace and dignity. Their feet and hands were small and exquisitely shaped. The hair of the male was shaved, except a patch on the back of the head, which was ornamented with beads and feathers, or with a colored deer's tail. Their ears were slit and stretched to an enormous size, causing the persons who had the cutting performed to undergo incredible pain. They slit but one ear at a time, because the patient had to lay on one side forty days for it to heal. As soon as he could bear the operation wire was wound around them to expand them and when they were entirely well, they were adorned with silver pendants and rings."[*]

[‡] History of United States, vol 2, page 95. George Bancroft.
[†] Annals of Tennessee, page 83.
[‡] Travels in North America, page 483.
[*] Lieutenant Henry Timberlake.

Cherokee-Iroquois Family Theory.

Philologists are of the opinion that the following tribes belong to the same family: Wyandottes, Tiontates, Attiwandarons, Tohotaenrats, Wenroronos, Mohawks, Oneidas, Onondagas, Cayugas, Senecas, Eries, Conestogas, Nottaways, Meherrins, Tuscaroras and Cherokees. The idea of the relationship of the Cherokees to the Iroquoian family is based on the similarity of certain words, as for instance:

English.	Mohawk.	Overhill Cherokee.
person	ongwe	yunwi
fire	otsira	atsira
water	awen	awa
stone	onenya	unuyu
arrow	kanon	kuni
pipe	kanonnawen	kanun-nawu
hand (arm)	oweya	uwayi
milk	unenta	ununti
five	wisk	hiski
fish	otconta	utsuti
ghost	oskenna	asgina
snake	ennatun	inadu[†]

Religion.

The religion of the Cherokees was an obscure polytheism. The sun, their superior deity, was called "The Apportioner," dividing time into day and night, giving the four seasons, besides being the traditional giver of the "devine fire" of their ancestors. Ranking second among their gods was the "Long man," the representative of water. To him they made adjurations in all of their ceremonies, as an intercessory spirit. In most of their ceremonies it was necessary to plunge into the water before the Great Spirit could be invoked. The "Red man" (the name derivative, possibly, from the rising moon), the representative of the east, held the third place in importance.

[†] Myths of the Cherokees, page 188. James Mooney in nineteenth annual report of Bureau of Ethnology.

William Potter Ross. Cherokee genealogy No. XVI—
$1^1 1^2 1^3 2^4 1^5$. Graduate from Princeton College. Principal
Chief of Cherokee Nation from August, 1866, to
November, 1867, and from November 11, 1872, to
November, 1875.

third place in importance. The stone was invoked by the conjuror in his attempt to find any lost article. Plants were sometimes addressed as deities. "Slanting eyes," a giant hunter, who lived in one of the great mountains of the Blue Ridge, and owned all of the game, was the patron saint of the hunter. Others were the "Little man," who lived in the thunder; the "Little people," fairies who dwelt in the rock cliffs; and in fact, they worshipped almost everything tangible and many "strange gods," conjured by a vivid imagery. Thus it will be seen that their pantheon was as extensive as that of ancient Rome.

The animistic gods should not be confounded with their common representatives that were encountered almost every day, but they were their great primogenitors, who now dwell in the upper world, and exercise a protective supervision over their kind. The gods were described as having certain symbolic colors, which were associated with the cardinal points of the compass: a red god was from the east and bestowed triumph and success; a white god from the south brought peace and happiness; the blue god from the north brought only defeat and trouble, while from the west the black god brought death, and above, brown, like a cloud, obscured all, but was propitious, as after clouds we expect sunshine. Yellow had the same significance as blue.

Conjurors.

The only semi-heriditary rights practiced among the Cherokees was that of the adoniska or conjurors. Their origin was so ancient that it was generally supposed that they were instituted shortly after the destruction of the earlier priesthood, who had appropriated the holy fire. The Cherokees believed implicitly that the conjurors could cause rain,[*] kill, disable or otherwise harm anyone who came under their displeasure,

---

[*] About the year of 1872 my father was passing through a neighborhood (on Spring Creek, some ten miles east of the newly built Missouri, Kansas & Texas Railroad), in which the Cherokee language was in general use. He came to a large crowd congregated at a school house. These people were very much depressed, as one of their number told my father that Terrapin, their conjuror, had just told them that the drouth[sic] that was then prevailing would last as long as the iron rails of the Missouri, Kansas & Texas Railroad stretched unbroken from north to south and stopped the rain clouds, as they could not pass over it. But a timely rain dispelled this delusion.

Dennis Wolf Bushyhead. Cherokee genealogy No. 1—
$1^1 1^2 3^3 1^4 1^5 2^6$. Principal Chief of the Cherokee Nation
from 1879 to January, 1888.

regardless of the distance between the conjuror and his victim; transform themselves into the semblance of any bird or animal at pleasure, then reassume their former shape and condition at will; divine the present or future and cure diseases or snake bite. It is a well known fact that they can handle the most venomous snakes with impunity, and if possible will prevent snakes from being killed. If anyone should kill a snake near the home of a conjuror, he is sure to incur his maledictions. The position of conjuror was much coveted, but, besides being generally handed down in one family, it was not easy to attain, as many of the formulas could only be imparted by a single rehearsal, during a certain moon, or a certain season, and then only by one of the opposite sex.[II] The formula for the cure of the bite of a snake could only be imparted during cold weather,[†] while the snakes were dormant.

Ceremonial Beads.
Beads were generally used in their devinations, some five or six being used. It was claimed that when they were first cast into a stream that they would sink, but in answer to the incantations of the conjuror they would rise to the top of the water and by their gyrations, waterbugwise, they would indicate the details sought.

Longevity.
"On account of the pure air which they breathed, the exercise of the chase, the abundance of natural productions which the country afforded, the delicious water which was always near, many Cherokees lived to a very advanced age."[‡]

Mortuary Customs.
"When a person was past recovery (to prevent pollution) they dug a grave, prepared a tomb, anointed the hair of the patient and painted his face, and when death ensued interment was immediately performed. After the third day the attendants at the funeral appeared at the council house and engaged in their ordinary pursuits, but the relatives lived in

[II] The conjurors were both male and female.
[†] My informant on this point was Mrs. William E. Chambers, a highly intelligent Cherokee lady, who is perfectly conversant with the Cherokee language and has much first hand knowledge of their customs.
[‡] History of the American Indians, page 226. James Adair.

retirement and moaned for some time."[§]

It was formerly the habit of the Cherokees to shoot all stock belonging to the deceased and they, together with his guns, bows and household utensils were buried with him, that he might be provided for in the next world. If one died upon a journey, hunt or war expedition, his companions erected a stage, upon which a notched log pen was built, in which the body was placed to secure it from wild beasts. When it was supposed that sufficient time had elapsed, so that nothing remained but the bones, they returned to the spot, collected these, carried them home and buried them with great ceremony.

"Sometimes heaps of stones were raised as monuments to the dead, whose bones they had not been able to 'gather to their fathers,' and everyone who passed by added a stone to the pile."[*] These aboriginal burial customs were entirely changed for those of their white neighbors by 1800.

Dances.

Almost without exception their dances were of a religious character, and were for the purpose of thanking, or imploring, their gods for favors. Their principal dance was the "green corn dance," which was a thanksgiving for their "staff of life." This was at roasting ear time, and it was invariably preceded by some three days by the "medicine dance," the principal feature of which was the drinking of a strong decoction of herbs, which acted as a violent emetic and chologogue. At the end of this dance the warriors, after scarifying their persons freely with the talons of an eagle or the claws of some beast "to let out the bad thickened blood of the cold season," as they claimed, plunged into a running stream, then presented themselves before the conjuror, who, holding the icacati between himself and the applicant, saw by the straight flame the happy omen, or, if the flame was bent, the doubting, fearing man, turned, rescarified himself and, muttering supplications to the Great Spirit, plunged again into the stream; then if, on the second visit to the conjuror, the flame still remained bent, his doom was sealed and he knew that he would never live to see another "medicine dance," He then plunged desperately into any war or feud that might exist and often, ere many

---

[§] Ibid, 126.
[*] Memoirs of Lieutenant Henry Timberlake, 1765.

moons waned, he was crowned with the halo of a great warrior and left to his family the heritage and memory of a hero.

Associated Charity.

"They had a particular method of relieving the poor, which ought to be ranked among the most laudable of their religious ceremonies. The headmen issued orders for a war dance, at which all of the fighting men of the town assembled. But here, contrary to all other dances, only one danced at a time, who, with a tomahawk in his hand, hopped and capered for a minute, and then gave a whoop. The music then stopped till he related the manner of his taking his first scalp. He concluded his narration and cast a string of wampum, wire, plate, paint, lead or anything he could spare upon a large bear skin spread for the purpose. Then the music again began and he continued in the same manner through all his warlike actions. Then another succeeded him, and the ceremony lasted until all the warriors had related their exploits and thrown presents upon the skin. The stock thus raised, after paying the musicians, was divided among the poor. The same ceremony was used to recompense any extraordinary measure."[*]

Legends.

Reverend Cephas Washburn, a Presbyterian missionary, who came among the "Western Cherokees" in 1820, gives in his "Reminiscenses" (which is the greatest and most authentic work on Indian sociology ever written), the substance of a conversation that he had with Ta-ka-e-tuh, a highly intelligent and philosophic Cherokee conjuror, in which, among other statements, Ta-ka-e-tuh said: "The earth was created, next to the sun, moon and stars; then man, then birds, then land animals, then fish and reptiles, and lastly vegetables and fruits, to be food for man and beast. The period of time occupied in the creation was six days, or rather six nights, after which was a day of rest, which gave rise to the division of time into periods of seven days."[†] In answer to a query as to their gods, he said: "There is one god, although our people believe in a great many ghosts (skillies)." At first there was one man and one woman created,[‡] the first human pair was red, and the

---

[*] History of Alabama, page 144. Albert J. Pickett.
[†] Genesis, chapter 11, verse 2.
[‡] Genesis, chapter 11, verses 7, 21 and 22.

14

varieties in color of the human race he accounted for by the influence of climate, except in the case of blacks. Black was a stigma on a man for a crime, and all of his descendants have been born black. The first human pair was placed in a most beautiful country, which spontaneously yielded delicious fruits, was adorned with delicate and fragrant herbs and flowers, enlivened and made delightful by the music of birds. It was so perfectly healthful that disease and death was unknown. Such was the whole earth at that happy time. At that time the human race lived far to the west on the other side of a very large salt lake. The days and nights were the same length; the temperature was always the same, neither too hot not too cold. The rain fell in gentle showers and only pleasant and refreshing breezes swept over the earth. There was no thunderings, lightnings or earthquakes. The birds were all sweet singers and could all sing in concert; the voices of all animals were sweetly harmonious. No harsh or unpleasant sound was heard on earth and every vegetable was pleasant and useful. All the animals that now exist existed then, except serpents and such as are a cross of different races, like the mule; that very many species of animals had ceased to exist. Then animals could understand each other's language and man could converse with all beasts, birds and fish.

The Creator often came down to earth and conversed most familiarly with man, and all the earth was peace, love and happiness. There was no increase of the human race during this happy period. The cause of the sad reverse was man's transgression of the law of his Maker. To this the man was tempted by the woman. One serpent was at first created, but he was not allowed to associate with the other creatures, but was shut up in a dark cavern in a rock. The first woman was walking by herself and as she passed the rock the serpent, singing in a sweetly soothing musical tone, attracted her notice and she paused to look and listen. Soon the serpent addressed her in a very friendly voice, then he opened a fissure in the rock and came into view. He held a long discourse with the woman, speaking with a voice so enchanting that, though what he proposed at first shocked her, yet at last he prevailed and induced her to violate the law of the Maker. He then induced her to tempt her husband; the serpent gave her power to prevail over the man and cause him to transgress the law of the Maker." On being asked what was the transgression he answered: "I do not know. Some say it was eating the fruit of a tree, which the Creator had forbidden. They

15

disobeyed the command of their Maker, and it makes no difference what that disobedience was. The Great Spirit was very angry and he punished them in a great many ways. The whole earth was changed, noxious weeds and thorns and poisonous vegetables were produced; dreadful storms, tempests and earthquakes took place and man was now exposed to unpleasant heat and then to freezing cold. The earth became unhealthy and all kinds of disease and plagues prevailed. The beasts were fighting each other and became unfriendly to man. The man and his wife often quarreled and were very unhappy and ever since all kinds of pains and suffering has prevailed everywhere and all have to die. Man, thus fallen and depraved, manifested no tendency to reform, but to progress from bad to worse, and this in a constantly accelerating rapidity. The life of man at that time was protracted to a very great number of years and this fact aided in multiplying crimes and carrying out schemes of wickedness and, of course, very greatly added to the miseries of life. At last man became so bad that God could bear it no longer, and determined to destroy all the race, except a single family. This one family alone of all the human race was good. The Creator told this family that he would bring a great flood of water and drown the whole world, and directed this family to build a very great raft and to make a house on the raft for the family and a storehouse for food, and then he told a pair of all kinds of animals that could not live in the water to go onto the raft with the good family, and so they were saved when the flood came. Before the flood the island on which we now live (meaning the entire Western continent) was down very deep in the great salt lake and God caused it to rise and water rolled to those parts of the earth where men and beasts were living, and so all that part of the world was overflowed to a great depth. The Great Spirit made great hollows or caverns in the earth and the water retired to these coverns, or, as many Red people believe, it may be that God, not needing the water any longer, he made it into rocks and minerals; at last, when every living thing, except those that could live in the water and those that were on the raft, was destroyed, God caused the waters to retire and the dry land appeared. The family and all the beasts left the raft and lived on the land as they had done before. It took a great many years for the earth to be populous, as it was before the flood. Since the flood the natural life of man has been much shorter."[*]

Reverend Daniel Sabin Buttrick.

Reverend Buttrick, a native of Windsor, Massachusetts, came as a missionary to the Cherokees in 1817. He lived among them until his death at Dwight Mission, Cherokee Nation, Indian Territory, on June 8, 1851. Soon after his advent among them, he commenced to study their language and succeeded to a degree, but was never able to preach the gospel to them in their own language.

In his intercourse with the people he became impressed with their myths. He gave a written interpretation of many of them and in writing out their statements he zealously gave the narrator or authority of each. Among these antiquities were the following:

Two Religions.

"With regard to the religious views of the Cherokees, it seems that, from time immemorial, they have been divided in sentiment. While a great part have been idolatrous, worshipping the sun, moon, stars and other gods,[†] a small portion have denied that system and taught the following: There are three beings above, who created all things and will judge all men. When these beings call any person out of the world they must die, and what kind of death these three think anyone should die, that kind of death is certain.[‡] The names of the beings are U-ha-li-te-qua, great, great, or the head of all power, great beyond expression; A-ta-no-ti, united or the place of uniting, and U-sqa-hu-la. These three beings are always one in sentiment and action, and always will be, and, being the governors and proprietors of all things, they sit on three white seats above and are the only objects of worship to whom alone all prayers are to be addressed. The angels are their messengers and come down to this earth to attend to the affairs of men.—Caty (Katie) Vann, Thomas Nutsawi."

---

[*] Reminiscences, Letter X. Cephas Washburn.
[†] See page 10.
[‡] They have here gotten their religions mixed and by superimposing their ancient idea of the personal accountability of the conjuror, they are vesting their apparent Hebraic God with attributes not generally accredited.

17

Ye-ho-wa.

"Ye-ho-wa was the name of a king who lived a great while ago. He was a man, and yet a spirit, a god, a very glorious being. His name was never to be spoken in common talk. This great king commanded them to rest every seventh day, and told them that if they should work on that day they should die, or some of their relatives. They were to hold their hands still (the palms up) and their talk must be about God. Ye-ho-wa was the most sacred name. None must speak it but persons appointed for the purpose, and they only on the Sabbath. God created the world in seven days.—Nutsawi."

Creation.

"The world was created at the time of the first new moon in autumn, with the fruits all ripe. The first new moon in autumn is therefore the great new moon, or Nu-ta-te-qua, and with it the year commences, as regards the feasts of the new moons; though the first new moon in spring begins the year with regard to the feast of first fruits, because then the fruits begin to come forward.—Yu-wi-yoki."

"The great new moon made its appearance in autumn, when the leaves began to fall.—Nutsawi."

"God made man, red, of red clay, and made the woman of one of his ribs.—Nettle."

"At first no snakes or weeds were poisonous. Poison was afterwards communicated to them.—Thomas Nutsawi."

"Soon after the creation one of the family was bitten by a serpent and died. All possible means was resorted to in order to restore life, but all in vain. Being overcome in this first instance, the whole race were doomed to follow, not only to death, but to misery afterwards, as it was supposed that that person went to misery.

"Another tradition says that soon after the creation a young woman was bitten by a serpent and died, and her spirit went to a certain place. The people were told that if they would get her spirit back to her body, that the body would live again, and they would prevent the general mortality of the body. Some young men, therefore, started with a box to catch the spirit. They went to a place and saw it dancing about, and at length caught it in the box and shut the lid, so as to confine it, and started back. But the spirit kept constantly pleading with them to open the box, so as to afford a little light, but they hurried on until they arrived near the place where the body was, and then, on account of her peculiar urgency, they removed the lid a very little, and out flew the spirit and was gone, and with it all their hopes of immortality.

"All were Indians, or red people, before the flood. They had also preachers and prophets before the flood. Their preachers would sometimes continue their discourses nearly all day, teaching the people to obey God. They also taught the children to obey their parents.

"They warned the people of the approaching flood, if they continued to disobey God, but said the world should not be destroyed by water but once; it would afterwards be destroyed by fire, when God would send first a shower of pitch, then a shower of fire to set everything in a flame. They also taught the people that after death the good and the bad would separate, the good would take a path which would lead them to a place of happiness, where it would be always light; but the bad would be urged along another path, which led to a deep gulf, over which lay a pole, with a dog at each end. They would be urged on to this pole, and the dogs, by moving it, would throw them off into the gulf of fire beneath. But if they got over, they would be transfixed with red hot bars of iron, and thus be tormented forever.

"The priests offered sacrifice with new fire, having a rack two or three feet high for an altar. A little before the flood men grew worse and worse, and, like some of the Cherokee young men now, grew worse by reproach and warning. Also, some infants were born with whole sets of teeth.—Nutsawi."

"At length God sent a messenger from above to warn the people of the flood unless they turned from their wickedness.

"God then told a man to make a house that would swim, and take his family and some of the different kinds of animals into it.—Raven."

"The rain commenced, and continued forty days and forty nights, while the water at the same time gushed out of the ground, so that as much came up as came down from the clouds.—Nutsawi, as also the Natcher."*

---

* You will notice that this narrative was also given by "the Natcher." This is the name by which the Cherokees knew the Natchez Indians, a part of whom settled in the Cherokee country after their dispersal by the French in 1732 (Louisiana, page 95. Le Page Dupratz, London, 1774). It is almost certain that the narrator, "the Natcher," was a Natchez Indian, and for this reason his story is possibly derived from the myths of his own tribe.

"The Natcher Indians also affirm further, that not a log or anything swam, but everything lay just as it was, so that the people could by no means save themselves from drowning.—Yuwi Yokh."

"The house or boat was raised upon the waters and bourne away. At length the man sent out a raven, and, after some time, sent a dove, which came back with a leaf in her mouth. Soon after this the man found the house (or boat) was resting on dry ground, on the top of the mountain. This being in the spring of the year, the family and all the animals left the boat, and the family descended to the bottom of the mountain and commenced their farming operations.—Nutsawi."

"Some time after the flood the people generally (the Indians excepted) determined to build a wall to reach the clouds, and proceeded till the wall was very high. They built this wall of stone (Nutsawi or, according to others, of wood; Shield Eater). At length the people became very much alarmed by seeing something black in the air above them; and also God was angry with them and spoiled their language, so that the people could not understand each other, and got into quarrels, and separated.—Nutsawi and Shield Eater."

"An old man, nearly a hundred years old, by the name of Kotiski, says that, when a small boy, he used to listen to the conversation of two very aged men, who would sometimes sit up and talk nearly the whole night; and among other things they told were the following: That there was a God, the father and the son; that these alone created all things; that they were always present, and knew all we said and did, and that the father sent the son to attend to and manage the affairs of the world.* Prayers were to be directed to these two, and also to Aquahami (Abraham), not however as a god, but as to their great father, who, though a man like themselves, was greater and wiser than themselves.

"When God created the world, He made a heaven or firmament about as high as the tops of the mountains, but this was too warm. He then created a second, which was also too warm. He thus proceeded until He had created seven heavens, and in the seventh fixed His abode.

---

* If this was one of the detailed accounts of Jewish history, then the Cherokees must have emigrated from Asia subsequent to the Christian era, as this plainly has reference to Jesus Christ, or it is a remarkable coincidence.

Samuel Houston Mayes. Cherokee genealogy No. XV—
$1^1 1^2 2^3 3^4 10^5$. Principal Chief of the Cherokee Nation from
November, 1895, to November, 1899.

"During some of their prayers they raise their hands to the first, second, third, fourth, fifth, sixth and seventh heaven, and then express their desires to God, who dwells there. But when they sung that special prayer designed for the morning of every day, they commenced with the third heaven, ascending to the fourth, fifth, sixth, seventh and then uttered their prayer to the Father and the Son, in substance as follows: 'Oh, God, thou hast created us, and hast the hearts of all in thy hands. We pray for thine aid, and for long life and health, Aquahami (Abraham) our father taught us to pray thus.' They then prayed to Abraham to take them into his arms. This prayer was sung every seventh morning, seven times, commencing a little before day, and about day-break they repaired to a stream of water and plunged entirely under four or seven times. The water washed away their heaviness, and God gave them comfort and joy in their hearts. They then prayed to Him to continue this joy in their hearts. On returning to the house they put their hands on the white ashes covering the coals, and rubbed their faces and breasts.[‡]

"The old men said that God created all things in six days and rested on the seventh; and therefore all must rest every seventh day, and meet at the town houses.

"The principal men called the people together at an early hour. No work was done except by women, who brought forward the food. The old men smoked, and the young men occasionally danced before them.

"At usual breakfast time the victuals were brought by fourteen women previously appointed, seven of whom waited on the men and seven on the women. The priests sat on their appropriate white seats; other men and boys on seats near the middle of the house; other men and boys on seats to the right, and the women and girls at the left. The victuals were set on the ground in dishes, before the several seats, and then the waiting women took their seats with the other females. The priest then arose and told the people that God, the Creator, had given them food, and that, by partaking of it, they would be refreshed, and then told them to eat. The repast being ended, the fourteen women took away the dishes. The leader of the dancers was then called forward. He arranged the company in single file; the leader followed by his wife, the next principal man and his wife, and so on, a man and his wife; or if a

---

[‡] May this not have been a fragment or idea from their ancient fire worship?

man had no wife, he was followed by a single female, who was a near relative, or of the same clan. This arrangement might form a number of circles in the house. Being thus arranged, while standing, the congregation was addressed by four priests successively. They occupied the great white middle seat. The eldest arose and spoke, holding a white wing of a fowl by the right side of his face. Together with various other instructions, he charged the people to love and be kind to one another. On concluding, the first took his seat, and handed the white wing to the next him and so on till all four had spoken. The white wing was then hung in a sacred place over their heads. The dance then commenced. Towards evening, all being again seated, the same women who had provided breakfast now brought forward the dinner (or supper) which was served as in the morning; and the night was wholly spent in dancing. None must sleep but small children. On the succeeding morning breakfast was brought, and after eating, all retired to their houses.

"The first man and woman were made of red earth, and therefore were red, and God told them that when they died they would turn to earth again. When God created the man and the woman, He told them to multiply.—Kotiski."

Creation.

"Big Pheasant relates the history of the creation, received from his grandmother and handed down from the old men before they had any knowledge from the whites. Beings from above came down and created the world and everything connected with it. They then called a council and created the man and gave him life. The man then fell into a sleep and the Lord took a rib from his side and made a woman, and gave her to the man. God instructed them about marriage and told them to multiply. This woman was the mother of all living people, i. e., of all nations. God directed them also not to use vulgar language or tell a lie, as these would be very wicked.—Big Pheasant."

The Book and the Bow.

"God gave the red man a book and paper and told him to write, but he merely made marks on the paper, and as he could not read or write, the Lord gave him a bow and arrows, and gave the book to the white man. A great while ago a part of the earth was burned, though it is

23

not known now how, or by whom, but it is said that other land was formed by washing it from the mountains.—Kotiski."[*]

Abraham.

"Aqua-ha-ye[†] (Abraham) was the greatest among their ancestors, but this is all that can be told of him."[‡]

Moses.

"The next man of greatest note among their early ancestors was by the name of Wasi (Moses). He was the greatest prophet and told them of things past, relative to the creation of the world, the history of mankind, and also told them things to come. He directed them how to consecrate their priests, how and when to celebrate their feasts, and how to attend to all their religious ceremonies and charged them to observe all he had commanded them forever.—Nutsawi."

The Flight.

"God loved their fathers and told them that they should be the father of all nations; and He gave them a country, though they had a great distance to travel to get to it. At length they started for their country, but when they started they were fleeing from their enemies. Who these enemies were, or where they lived, it is not now known. When they started they soon came to a great water, and because God loved their fathers, He told their leader (his name they do not know) to strike the water with a staff and it should divide until they passed through and then come together, so that their enemies could not follow to injure them. Their leader did this. He went forward striking the water and it parted so that all went through safely, and then the water came back and stopped their enemies. They then entered a vast wilderness.

---

[*] This, as many of their legends, was palpably, pitiably modern.
[†] Properly A-qua-ha-mi.
[‡] His authority for this statement is not given, but it was most probably Nutsawi.

The Law on the Tablet of Stone.

"Some time after they entered this wilderness they came to a high mountain, and God came down upon the mountain, and their leader went up and conversed with God, or rather, as their fathers said, with the Son of God, as it was said to be the Son of God that came down on the mountain, and the top of the mountain was bright like the sun. There God gave their leader a law written on a smooth stone. The reason of this being written on stone was as follows, viz: God gave our first parents a law to be handed down verbally to posterity. But when their language was destroyed and men began to quarrel and kill each other, they forgot this law, and therefore God wrote His law now on a stone, a smooth slate stone, that it might not be lost. Their leader also received other instructions from God which He wrote on skins.

The Ark of the Covenant.

"God also directed their leader to erect a certain building, to be covered with a cloth made of deer's hair and turkey feathers. This was to be set up when they rested and taken down and carried when they journeyed. God also directed them to repeat or chant certain sentences every morning at or about daylight and before going to sleep at night.

Holy Fire.

"In this wilderness God gave them their holy fire from heaven. This they ever kept for burning sacrifices and holy purposes, and though, when they came to this continent they left it behind, yet in a miraculous manner they had it brought over the great water and kept it, till on a certain occasion their enemies came upon them and destroyed the house in which it was kept. After that they were obliged to make new fire for sacred purposes by rubbing two pieces of dry wood together, with a certain weed called anagestaluga or light bearer,* dry, between them. After constant rubbing for some time this took fire together with the wood, and this fire was used for religious purposes.[†]

---

* Solidago rigida, or golden rod.
[†] The narrator of this long story is not given. It was most probably given by Shield Eater.

25

"When their enemies destroyed the house in which this holy fire was kept, it was said that the fire settled down into the earth, where it still lives, though unknown to the people. The place where they lost this holy fire is somewhere in one of the Carolinas.[‡]—Inata (Snake)."

"This new fire, made by friction, like the original holy fire, must not be used for any common purpose (except when made especially to supply the nation with new fire). No torch must be lighted by it, nor a coal taken from it for common use. After the sacrifice was burned and the ceremonies ended for which the fire was made, it was delivered to some one to keep.—Shield Eater or T. Smith."

"Originally they had twelve tribes but on account of disobedience with regard to marriage it was resolved to have but seven.[§]

"In their journeys through the wilderness, the tribes marched separately and also the clans. The clans were distinguished by having feathers of different colors fastened to their ears. They had two great standards, one white and one red. The white standard was under the control of the priests and used for civil and religious purposes; but the red standard was under the direction of the war priests for purposes of war or alarm. These were carried when they journeyed, and the white standard in front of the building above mentioned (the ark), when they rested. The priests had trumpets, also, for their own particular use.

"In going through this wilderness they had two waters to cross, between the first and the last river, before getting to their country. These two their leader struck, as he had done the first, and the water stopped so that the children could wade through. But their whole journey through this wilderness was attended with great distress and danger. At one time they were beset by the most deadly kind of serpents which destroyed a great many of the people, but at length their leader shot one with an arrow and drove them away.[*]

"Again they were walking along in single file, when the ground

---

[‡] This is one of the constant repetitions of the narrators' attempts to localize their stories, as the mind of man constantly queries, where and why?

[§] This recurrant[sic] story of the twelve tribes (or clans), although these were not synonymous terms, but had their origin in the lax and incompetent methods of interpreters and translators, were palpable references to the descendants of the sons of Jacob (Genesis, chapter 44, verse 28.

[*] Most probably an adaptation of the story of the brazen serpent. Numbers, chapter 21, verses 6 and 9.

cracked open and a number of people sunk down and were destroyed by the earth closing upon them.

"At another time they came nigh perishing for water. Their head men dug with their staves in all the low places but could find no water. At length their leader found a most beautiful spring coming out of a rock.

"They were a great many years in getting through the wilderness and many of the people died. They never could have got through, the dangers were so great, if God had not helped them.

"When they came to the land which God had given to their fathers, they had a large river to cross. This had been told them all along. But when they came to this river their leader struck it with his stick and the water above stopped so that all the children could wade through. After they had crossed they camped on the other side and named the place Tahmitoo.

"They had then to engage in wars—and on one occasion their leader caused the sun to stand still and thus lengthened the day, that they might destroy their enemies. And at another time the Lord destroyed their enemies by sending a hail storm upon them. Some of the hailstones being as large as a hominy mortar.[†]—Shield Eater, Nutsawi."

"In ancient times the Indians always had their places of worship near a river or creek, or on the bank of a lake, or on the seashore.—Thomas Nutsawi, Deer in the Water."

"The Indians never used to eat a certain sinew in the thigh. The name of this sinew in Cherokee is u-wa-sta-to. Some say that if they eat of the sinew, they will have cramp in it on attempting to run. It is said that once a woman had cramp in that sinew and therefore none must eat it.—Nutsawi."

The foregoing translations of Cherokee myths were gathered by Rev. Daniel Sabin Buttrick, who was thoroughly convinced by these relations, the writings of Elias Boudinot and the "History of the American Indians," by James Adair, that the Indians were of Asiatic

---

[†] A hominy mortar was ordinarily a section of an oak tree trunk, about eighteen or twenty inches in diameter and two feet in length, which was hollowed out, either on the side or in one end, to hold the corn to be made into hominy with a pestle, which is a smooth rounded stick of heavy wood, generally made from heart wood of the oak, its dimensions being about five inches thick and five feet in length, one end being slightly larger than the other. The corn is pounded until it is of the proper consistency, then boiled with water to render it edible.

William Charles Rogers. Cherokee genealogy No. 1—$1^1 1^2 2^3 5^4 4^5 4^6$. Principal Chief of the Cherokee Nation from November, 1903, to the present time.

origin and were descendants of the Jews.

But Reverend Buttrick seems to have overlooked the history of Christian Priber, that was given in the same volume as were Adair's specious deductions from Semitic appearing customs.

I have given you only a few references to the apparent biblical analogies, although almost every statement of these several myths are coincidental with the stories of the Old Testament.

The well intentioned student of folk lore has often with rapt enthusiasm pursued the ignis fatuus of Cherokee myths, seeing through them, down the mystic trail of time, until almost the footfalls of his Jewish ancestors, could by his intent mind be conjured.

But the facts are too plain: Priber told the Cherokees the several Bible stories in the nine years between 1736 and 1745. The Cherokees, forgetting the primal origin, necessarily localized them so that they, themselves, could better understand them; and retold them to the early Moravian, Presbyterian, Baptist and Methodist missionaries from 1803 to 1830.

CHRISTIAN PRIBER.

Christian Priber, a Jesuit, reputed to have been a German acting in the interest of the French, came among the Cherokees in 1736. A scholarly man, he was the master of the Greek, Latin, French, German, English and Spanish languages.

Soon after his arrival among the Cherokees he cast aside the gown of the cleric, assumed the habiliments of the Cherokees and took to wife one of their women.

In a very short time he had acquired such a knowledge of their language that it enabled him to write a Cherokee-French dictionary.

He persuaded the Cherokees to elect one of their leading men as emperor and he became his secretary. In this guise he carried on quite a deal of diplomatic correspondence with the neighboring English and French colonies.

He drew up the form of a regularly organized government and for nine years was the most potent figure in Cherokee affairs, a place to which his judgment, courage, learning and polished manners well qualified him.

At one time an officer from the colony of South Carolina was dispatched to Great Telequ (Great Tahlequah or Tellico) in Tennessee, which at that time was the capitol of the Cherokees and the residence of Priber, to arrest him on the charge of being a French emissary. The Cherokees refused to allow him to be taken from their town and were desirous of executing the officer, but Priber interceded for him and furnished him a safe escort to his home colony.

He was a citizen and continuous resident in the Cherokee nation for nine years but while on a trip to the French Fort Toulouse in 1745, to negotiate with some Muskogee Chiefs, he was surprised and captured by the English and taken to Fredericka, Georgia where he was put into prison.

Soon after his incarceration the colonial authorities determined to rid themselves of him by placing a quantity of powder in a room adjacent to that in which he was held. Priber's prison room had a dirt floor and the door was kept open so that the guard could watch him. The guard had been notified that at a certain signal he was to run over a slight declivity and escape injury. Priber had so ingratiated himself with the guard that he told him when the explosion was to occur and besought him to also save himself by flight.

At the signal the guard ran away and the explosion occurred. Priber's would-be executioners hurried to the scene of the explosion to find his mangled remains, but on arriving they found him arising from the ground with his hands over his ears. He explained to them that on account of the fact that the concussion of powder was always upward, that he lay prone on his stomach on the dirt floor with his hands over his ears to break the force of the concussion and that the building was blown from over him.

The next attempt at his life was more certain. He was starved to death.

His Cherokee dictionary—has since his death—been lost to the world.[*]

Cherokee Intermarriage.

In the racial blends of the Cherokees very little Spanish or French blood ever became a part; and today the great preponderance of foreign blood in the native of the old Cherokee Nation is English and

---

[*] History of American Indians, James Adair, pp. 240-243; History of Alabama, Albert Pickett, pp. 271-277; History of Georgia, Vol. 22, W. B. Stevens, pp. 104-107.

Scotch-Irish.

The first white man that is known to have married into the Cherokee tribe was Cornelius Dougherty, an Irish trader from Virginia, who married a full blood Cherokee woman in 1690[||].

From this time forward there was a steady increase of White intermarried citizens in the Cherokee country.

In 1738-39 smallpox broke out among the Cherokees and destroyed one-half of the tribe[†].

With the consent of the Cherokees, the English built Forts Prince George, Loudon and Dobbs in the Cherokee country in 1756. The ostensible purpose of the building of these forts was that they should serve as a part of a line of British forts erected to stop the encroachments of the French. They were garrisoned with Scotch Highlanders.

The indignities heaped on the Cherokees by the English, whom they helped in their war against the Shawnees, in 1756 at last caused the Cherokees to seek reprisals[‡].

They commenced war on the settlements; captured Fort Loudon[§] on August 8th, 1760; but were eventually defeated and caused to sign a treaty of peace on November 19th, 1761.

War soon broke out afresh between the Cherokees and their White neighbors and continued intermittingly for thirty years longer.

The treaties between the Cherokees and the colonies, and later the United States, were in almost every instance for the purpose of inducing the Indians to part with a part of their lands.

[||] Haywood. Natural and Aboriginal History of Tennessee, page 233.
[†] North Carolina Colonial Records, vol. V, pages 320 and 321.
[‡] Nineteenth annual report of the Bureau of Ethnology, part 1, page 41.
[§] Fall of Fort Loudon, by Charles Egbert Craddock.

CHEROKEE ALPHABET.

CHARACTERS SYSTEMATICALLY ARRANGED WITH THE SOUNDS

D	R	T	ꭹ	Oᴼ	i
a	e	i	o	oo	v
ꮝ	ꭴ	ꭺ	y	A	J	E
ga	ka	ge	gi	go	gu	gv
ꮼ	ꭾ	ꮂ	F	Г	ꮟ
ha	he	hi	ho	hu	hv
W	ꭿ	ꮈ	G	M	ꭴ
la	le	li	lo	lu	lv
ꭼ	ꮅ	H	ꮍ	y
ma	me	mi	mo	mu
Ɵ	t,	ꭸ	G	h	Z	ꮗ	ꮆ
na	nha	ne	nah	ni	no	nu	nv
ꮋ	ꮼ	ꮼ	ꮼ	ꮼ	ꮼ
qua	que	qni	quo	qua	quv
ꭴ	ꮝ	ꮇ	ꮞ	ꮌ	ꭱ
s	sa	se	si	so	su	sv
Ꮏ	W	ꮝ	ꭲ	ꮧ	ꭲ	V	S	ꮣ
da	ta	de	t	di	ti	do	du	dv
ꭿ	ꭷ	L	O	ꮛ	ꮵ	P
dla	tla	tle	cle	tlo	tlu	tlv
G	ꮴ	ꮯ	K	ꮷ	Cꭷ
tsa	tse	tsi	tso	tsu	tsv
G,	ꮺ	ꮎ	ꮝ	ꭷ	ꮜ
wa	we	wi	wo	wu	wv
ꮒ	ꮹ	ꮝ	ꮅ	ꮁ	B
ya	ye	yi	yo	yu	yv

SOUNDS REPRESENTED BY VOWELS

A as a in father, or short as a in rival.
E as a in hate, or short as e in met.
I as i in pique, or short as i in pin.
O as o in note, but as approaching to aw in law.
U as oo in moon, or short as u in pull.
V as u in but, nasalized.

CONSONANT SOUNDS.

G, is sounded hard approaching to k; sometimes before e, i, u and v, its sound is k. D has a sound between the English d and t; sometimes, before o, u, and v its sound is t; when written before l and s the same analogy prevails.
All other letters as in English.
Syllables beginning with g, except ga have sometimes the power of k; syllables when written with tl, except tla sometimes vary to dla.

32

Cherokee Land Cessions.

The relinquishments of land by the Cherokee tribe from 1721 to 1900, are as follows:

	Acres	Monetary Consideration	Stipulations
1721	1678720$		Cherokee boundary line fixed.
1755 Nov. 24,	5526400		Treaty with South Carolina.
1768 Oct. 14,	544000		Treaty with Great Britain.
1770 Oct. 18,	5888000		
1772	500480	5000 or 6000	Treaty with Virginia.
1773 June 1,	672000		Treaty with Great Britain.
1775 Mar. 17,	17312000	5000	Sale to Richard Henderson, et al.
1777 May 20,	1312640		War indemnity.
1777 July 20,	3951360		War indemnity.
1783 May 31,	1056000		Treaty with Georgia.
1785 Nov. 28,	4083840		War indemnity. First treaty with United States.
1791 July 2,	2660480	1000 annuity	
1798 Oct. 2,	984960	1000 annuity and $5000	
1804 Oct. 28,	86400	1000 annuity and $5000	
1805 Oct. 25,	5195520	3000 annuity and $14000	Secret grant of three square miles to Double-head and two tracts of a square mile each to Talonteeskee for their influence in helping to negotiate this treaty.
1805 Oct. 27,	800	1600	

		Acres	Monetary Consideration	Stipulations
1806	Jan. 7,	4397440	10000 Grist mill and cotton cleaning mill	$100 life annuity to Black Fox.
1816	March 22,	94720		
1816	Sept. 14,	2197120	65000	
1817	July 8,	651520	6500	3020800 acres set aside in Missouri territory for the Cherokees that were then residing west of Mississippi river.
1819	Feb. 27,	3802240		Additional land to equalize cession to "Western Cherokees," also twelve square miles set aside to be sold for a school fund.
1828	May 28,	3020800	10000 school fund	Exchanged "Western Cherokee land in Arkansas Territory (late Missouri Territory) for 14690079.73 acres west of said territory, also $1200 to Thomas Graves and $500 to George Guess
1835	Dec. 29,	7882240	5000000	$200000 of this was added to the National school fund.
1866	May 10,	3400	5000	This land was the "Old Settler" Cherokee Agency in Pope County, Arkansas. Knowledge of this treaty was kept from the Cherokees by their delegation.

		Acres	Monetary Consideration	Stipulations
1866	July 19,	1234294		The land ceded is now in Cherokee and Crawford Counties, Kansas.
1872	June 5,	1466167	1026216.90	Osage reservation.
1872	June 5,	100141	72820.51	Kaw reservation.
1876	April 10,	230014.04	161900.828	Pawnee reservation.
1878	May 27,	90710.89	43078.601	Nez Perce reservation.
1881	Mar 3,	101894.31	48389.607	Ponca reservation.
1881	Mar 3,	129113.20	61315.858	Oto-Missouri reservation.
1893	March 4,	8144682.91	8595736.12	Cherokee Outlet.
1900	Apr. 9,	4420067.73		Cherokee Nation allotted.
		89420165.08		

Sequoyah and Hicks.

In about the decade of 1760-1770, two remarkable half blood Cherokee boys were born in the Cherokee country. One Sequoyah, latterly called George Guess.

The other boy, born about the same time, was the son of Nathan Hicks and his wife, who was a daughter of Broom, an influential Cherokee subchief.

It was at Broom's town that the first known written law of the Cherokees was promulgated; the date thereof being September 11th, 1808.[*]

Sequoyah lived to be about seventy-five years of age and never acquired a word of the English language. While still a boy he was afflicted with anasarca, which left him a cripple for life; he was a drunkard from early manhood until he was about forty years of age.

Charles Hicks was gifted and talented, early in life he became the political leader of the Cherokees; but today the name of Sequoyah is known the world over, and I have the distinction of introducing Charles

[*] Laws of the Cherokee Nation, compiled in 1852, page 3.

Hicks to you.

Charles Hicks was born about 1760 in the Cherokee country; his neighbors, his friends and his known relatives, with the exception of his father, all being Cherokees and speaking that language exclusively. There were no schools in the Cherokee country before 1801 and we have no knowledge of his having been sent away to school, but by 1808[†] we find that this most reticent of men; this man who from 1810 or earlier[‡] while actually Second Chief and exercising at one and the same time practically all of the legislative and executive functions of the Cherokee government, always signed his name to executive documents as Charles Hicks, or later as Ch. R. Hicks, without appending any official designation.

He joined the church of the United Brethren at Spring Place and was baptized on April 16th, 1813; at which time the missionaries, as was their wont, conferred upon him the middle name of Renatus, or the renewed; Charles Renatus Hicks.

Chief Charles Hicks.

In October, 1817, he was described as follows: "He is a halfbreed Cherokee, about fifty years of age. He has very pleasant features and an intelligent countenance. He speaks English language with the utmost facility and with great propriety. I was exceedingly surprised that a Cherokee should be able to obtain so extensive a knowledge of English words as he possesses. He reads better than one-half of the white people and writes an easy hand. For thirty years he has been, as occasions required, an interpreter for the United States. As a man of integrity, temperance and intelligence, he has long sustained a most reputable character."[*]

A description of the residence of Chief Hicks was given at the same time, as follows: "It is made of hewn pine logs, is twenty-feet by eighteen, two stories high with a double piazza the whole length of the house, ornamented with handrails and banisters, and covered with a good roof of shingles, which is not usually the fact in the western country."[†]

[†] Laws of the Cherokee Nation, compilation 1852, page 3.
[‡] See signature as interpretor to the United States-Cherokee Treaty of October 2, 1798.
[*] Memoirs of Elias Cornelius, Chapter III.
[†] Memoirs of Elias Cornelius, Chapter III.

The death of Charles Hicks was in 1827, and his last known signature was attached to a council bill of November 28, 1826.

SEQUOYAH.

Sequoyah, the loving mother named her baby. Named him, just as any Anglo Saxon mother might name her son John or William. This was the custom among the Cherokees and they did not name their children on account of some occurrence or resemblance, as many uninformed ones simply surmise.

Take down your dictionary and you will find that even the good old names of John and William each have their archaic derivations. In the same manner, so, most probably did the name Sequoyah have somewhere in the dim and distant past a definite original meaning, but analytic philology among the Cherokees was almost an unknown art. The name was possibly derived from siqua, a hog and ayatla, within, or he is within; literally a hog in a pen; but even this derivation is only conjectural.

The name of the individual gave no indication of the relationship of the person bearing it to the other members of his or her family. The only kinship distinguishable was that of the clan. The individual always belonged to the clan that his or her mother belonged to. Sequoyah's mother belonged to the Paint clan and for that reason Sequoyah also belonged to the Paint clan.

Sequoyah was most probably born about 1770. He was born in the old Cherokee country, within one of the present states of North Carolina, South Carolina, Tennessee, Georgia or Alabama, but the exact location of his birth place is not known.

His father is reputed to have been a Suabian peddler from the now extinct town of New Ebenezer, Georgia, which had been founded as a refuge for the persecuted Moravians of Germany. His name as it was recalled many years afterwards, so as to bestow the patronymic on his illustrious son, sounded something like Gist. He was an obscure wanderer, a part of the adventurous flotsam of the border of civilization.

During his most probably short stay among the Cherokees he, as was the universal custom among all local White men of that period, chose a wife from among the Indians. She, according to the standards of her people of that day, was his wife. She cooked his meals, kept his

37

home, was his willing servant, she loved and cherished and bore children for him. He hunted for sustenance and pleasure, traded for profit or idled; it made no difference to her, he was her husband and her idol. Very often he wantonly deserted his wife and family, and in this instance, this was the case. German he was, Gist was possibly his name, a vagabond with the morals of his kind, no more is known of him.

Sequoyah was born after his father had deserted his mother. His mother spoke the Cherokee language only and the son never learned any of the English language.[*]

Of his boyhood we know nothing more than that he was a victim of a hydrarthritic trouble of the knee joint, commonly called "white swelling." This affliction caused a slight lameness that characterized him during life.[†]

He was about five feet eight in height, slim and sinewy. Years rounded his form but never imposed corpulency on him. He was of a light sallow complexion and had grey eyes.

In dress he clung to the customs of his people, wearing the turban, hunting shirt, leggings and moccasins. The turban was a strip of cloth or a small shawl deftly twisted about the head; the hunting shirt was a loose sack coat and was originally made of buckskin, but after about 1820 the Cherokee hunting shirt was almost always made from striped home spun woolen cloth that was made on the private looms by the Cherokee women. These striped hunting shirts were as distinctive with the Cherokees as were the tartans with the Scotch. The Cherokees that settled west of the Mississippi River in the latter part of the eighteenth century adopted a short hunting shirt that would only reach to about the second joint of the index finger and the Eastern Cherokee clung to the longer pattern that extended to his knee and in cold weather he wore a girdle around his waist to better confine his hunting shirt. The ground color of the cloth that these hunting shirts were made from was either brown, dark blue or black and the stripes were generally a grouping of red and blue or red, white and blue; the longitudinal stripe thus formed was generally about two inches wide. The cloth was always the native homespun.

The leggings were originally made of tanned buck skin but by

---

[*] Cherokee Advocate, Vol. I, No. 5; Oct. 26th, 1844.
[†] Cherokee Advocate, Col. I, No. 40; June 26th, 1845.

1820 they were almost universally made from homespun cloth, similar in weave to the material from which the hunting shirts were made but always of solid colors, either brown, dark blue or black.

The moccasins were always made from tanned buck skin and were often ornamented with bead work.

Sequoyah's homes were always the conventional log cabin covered with riven boards "chinked* and daubed" with clay and with a huge fire place on one side.

He first became a blacksmith, then a silversmith, but in either his usefulness was often marred by his love of liquor.

Sequoyah's first wife was Sallie of the Bird clan and his second wife sad Sallie U-ti-yu of the Blind Savannah clan.

His four children by his first wife were:

Teesey Guess, who married U-ti-yu and Rebecca Bowl. He was born in 1789 and died September 17th, 1867. His second wife, Rebecca Bowl, was the daughter of Bowl, who was the leader of the band of Cherokees that emigrated from Mussel Shoals, on Tennessee River, to the St. Francis River country (now southeast Missouri) in 1794; moved to Petit Jean Creek on the south side of Arkansas River in the winter of 1811-1812, finally removed to Texas in 1822 and became the leader of the Texas Cherokees. While resisting expulsion from Texas—Bowl who was then eighty-three years of age, was killed on July 16th, 1839 by Captain Robert Smith of the Texas volunteers.

Sequoyah's second child by Sallie was George Guess, who lived to be grown but died without descent. Richard or Chusaleta, the fourth child and third son, also lived to be grown and died without descent.

Sequoyah's third child by Sallie was his daughter Polly, who married Flying and Thomas Brewer. She only had one child, Annie, who married Joseph Griffin and was the mother of Ti-du-gi-yo-sti.

Sequoyah had three children by his second wife, U-ti-yu, the eldest of whom was A-yo-gu Guess, who married George Starr and they were the parents of one son, Joseph Starr, who was born on December 25, 1873, and died without issue in 1899.

---

* "Chinks" were generally short split sticks of wood that were fitted as well as possible in the cracks between the logs, so as to give a better foundation for the clay. A house properly "chinked and daubed" could be made as comfortable as a brick, stone or frame house.

Sequoyah's residence in Sequoyah County, Oklahoma. (This photograph was made in 1912.)

Sequoyah's second child by U-ti-yu was Oo-loo-tsa, a daughter, who left no descent.

Sequoyah's third child by his second wife was Gu-u-ne-ki, who married Tsu-du-li-tee-hee or Sixkiller and had one daughter, Araminta Sixkiller.

Sequoyah's eldest son, Teesey, had three children by his first wife and three by his second wife. His oldest child by his first wife, U-ti-yu, was George Guess, who married a Girty and they were the parents of two children, the elder of whom was Mary Guess, who married George Mitchell and Andrew Russell, and by the latter was the mother of one child only, George W. Russell, who was born on July 18th, 1880, and married Minnie Holston.

Tessey Guess's second and third children by his first wife was respectively Richard and Joseph Guess, both of whom lived to be grown but died without issue.

Tessey Guess's children by Rebecca, his second wife, was first, Sallie, who married William Fields, whose Cherokee name was Tu-noo-ie. They had one daughter, Susie Fields, who married Levi Toney and they were the parents of, consecutively: Calvin Hanks Toney, Cicero Davis Toney, Margaret Toney and the twins Catherine and Sallie Toney.

Teesey's[sic] Guess's second child by Rebecca was a son, Joseph Guess, who lived to be grown but died without issue.

Teesey Guess's third child by Rebecca was Catherine Guess. She was born in 1851 and married on March 11th, 1867, Joseph Downing, who was three years her senior. He died on March 20th, 1897. They were the parents of five children, as follows:

Nannie Downing, born February 1st, 1878; married January 21st, 1898, Richard H. Bowl.

Lucile Downing born July 28th, 1881.

Edward Downing born March 22nd, 1883.

Sequoyah Downing was born December 16th, 1887.

Maud Downing born February 13th, 1890.

I have given the foregoing detailed statement of the descent from Sequoyah for the reason that he has already become to a degree a mythical personage and claims of descent from him has been for years and is at this time most ridiculous assumptions.

In an article in the September, 1870, number of Harper's Monthly Magazine on page 547 Colonel William A. Phillips, late commander of the "Third Indian Home Guards," a federal regiment composed principally of Cherokees, asserted that one of the sons of Sequoyah "served as a private soldier in the Union army in the late war." This was an error as all of the descendants of Sequoyah that were old enough to be in the army were in the Confederate service. His son, Teesey, was third sergeant of Captain John Porum Davis's company of Cherokee Mounted Volunteers.

These claims of descent from Sequoyah remind me of an old White man that I knew a few years ago who always stoutly insisted that Pocahontas, of John Smith fame, was his great grandfather.

The prevalent idea among the Cherokees of his day was that the written page actually talked to the white man.

Sequoyah noticing the strange cabalistic marks, conceived the idea that each one represented a word, but upon getting an English book and counting the different marks therein, he soon saw that their number was inadequate to the expression of a language. In 1809 his meditations culminated in the idea that probably each mark represented a sound. To test this, he scratched with his knife on a stone the character G, naming it wa, and E which he called gu. This demonstrated to him the probable feasibility of his idea, as by the marks and the sounds that he applied to them, he represented the Cherokee word wagu, which is their word for cow.* At the same time he scratched out three other figures to which he gave the sequent sounds of tsa, qui and li, this being the Cherokee word for horse. By this time he was satisfied with the correctness of his idea. Henceforward he continued to multiply, eradicate and change marks, to each of which he gave distinctive sounds.

The form of many of the characters he adopted from the English, although he misjudged their proper use in the original. As he became more absorbed in his work he grew correspondingly more abstemious in his use of liquor. He announced to his friends that he was going to make the "leaf"* talk to the Indian as well as to the White man. This, to them, was incredible, as they had no standard to judge by and it exposed him to some ridicule, although not enough to keep him from being one of the signers of the United States-Cherokee treaty of September 14th, 1816.

---

* This Cherokee word was derived from the Spanish word for a cow, as they had learned this Spanish name for the strange beast that DeSoto's expedition had introduced among them.
* They at that time called a paper a leaf.

Only men of considerable merit were accorded this honor, as they were regularly elected for this purpose. His manuscripts were pieces of bark, his pencil a piece of charcoal.[†] At one time his wife, becoming disgusted at his apparently useless dronery, consigned his entire work of several years to flames. On his return he found his work destroyed, and after remonstrating with her, he again set to work and in a short time produced a small bundle of bark manuscript, which he assured his wife was identical with the several armloads that she had destroyed. This only helped to confirm her opinion of his dementia. The syllabary was finished in 1824.[‡]

It was the only alphabet in the whole world to be finished by one man and was so complete that anyone understanding the Cherokee language, could, upon learning the eighty-six letters of this syllabary, read and write correctly. As a witness to its perfection may be adduced the fact that no change, either by addition or elimination, has ever been found necessary.

He called his little daughter, A-to-ku, to him and while his anxious wife watched them he explained to the child the sound of each character and in a few days the poor woman not only had a husband whose sanity she doubted but her daughter claimed that she could make the leaf talk. The conjurers or medicine men were called in, and they, after swimming their beads and going through their incantations, declared that Sequoyah and A-to-ku were possessed of the evil spirits and should be killed.[*] The town chief (among whose other functions was that of justice and arbiter) of the community in which Sequoyah lived was George Lowry, a half blood Scotch-Cherokee, a man who spoke

[†] "I recollect very well the first intimation I had of the attempt of Sequoyah to invent an alphabet for the Cherokee language. In the winter of 1822-23 I was traveling with an intelligent Cherokee, (W. Hicks), who is now the Principal Chief of the Nation, on a road leading by the residence of Sequoyah. I had never heard of him until my companion pointed to a certain cabin on the wayside and observed, 'There in that house resides Sequoyah, who has been for the last year attempting to invent an alphabet. He has been so intensely engaged in this foolish undertaking, that he has neglected to do any other labor and permitted his farm to be overrun with weeds and briars.'" Elias Boudinot in Cherokee Phoenix, and afterdwards[sic] copied in the Cherokee Advocate, Vol. I, No. 5, October 26th, 1844.
[‡] Cherokee Advocate, Vol. I, No. 5, October 26th, 1844.
[*] This proceeding was in accordance with the old tribal customs, and although the Cherokees had adopted regular and more humane laws, the edicts and devinations of the conjurers still held sway in some remote districts.

both the Cherokee and English languages, had a fair English education, and had the love and respect of his neighbors on account of his wisdom and probity.[†]

In order to confirm the edict of the medicine men it was necessary to secure the assent of the town chief. After having examined Sequoyah and the child as to their ability to make the "paper talk," Lowry said that it was his opinion that they were possessed of the spirits and that possibly they should be killed. But at the same time he said that he did not wish to pass on the death penalty finally until a council had been held, that a popular verdict might be had. This gave general satisfaction. Ordinarily the older men in the community would have been called for such deliberations, but Lowry requested the young and implacable warriors of the Chicamauga[‡] towns to constitute this council. These were men that were continually at war, professional warriors, and did not live in the immediate neighborhood, as the nearest of their five towns was located forty miles north of Willstown, the home of Lowry. These men were to sit on the jury to try a man that had the reputation of having been bewitched—the same crime that had been so summarily suppressed in New England.

They assembled; Lowry reiterated to them that Sequoyah and A-to-ku were most probably possessed of the spirit and that it behooved them to look closely into this case and try to ascertain its merits, as it might possibly be that it was the Good Spirit that had sent him to bless the people and that is such was the fact and they voted to kill him the Good Spirit would most probably be very angry with them and blight the nation. The inquisition began, the warriors listened to the master and within one week each and everyone could read and write. By this stroke Sequoyah had thrown around him the proudest and fiercest aegis that ever escorted an original instructor.

He then established a school at his home, having for scholars aged grandparents, their children and grandchildren, grave missionaries, painted warriors who boasted between lessons of their bravery and prowess, white and Cherokee traders, many opulent and accomplished, cunning medicine men, who had lately been his most dangerous enemies,

---

[†] The position of town chief at this time was going out of existence and in a very few years it together with almost all of the other aboriginal Cherokee customs fell into disuse.
[‡] Chicamauga is from the Choctaw-Chickasaw word, aiachukma, meaning the good place.

and half breeds, proud and imperious. They finished their educations generally in three or four days, and seldom more than a week. He afterwards visited other neighborhoods on his mission of education. After about a year's work in the Cherokee Nation, "East," all of the Cherokees that cared to had mastered his syllabary, and Sequoyah visited the Cherokees who were then living on their reservation between the Arkansas and White Rivers, in Arkansas Territory. He shortly afterwards removed his family to that locality, which was then known as the Cherokee Nation, "West."

The National council of the Cherokee Nation, "East," voted a silver medal to Sequoyah. It was made under the supervision of John Ross (who had been President of the National Committee when the award was voted) in Washington, D. C., where Ross was serving as delegate for the Cherokee Nation, "East." This medal bore on one side a bust, surrounded with the inscription in English "Presented to George Gist by the General Council of the Cherokee Nation, for his ingenuity in the invention of the Cherokee alphabet." On the reverse side was a couple of pipes with stems crossed and encircled by the same inscription in Cherokee. It was intended that it should be presented to him in council, but on learning that Sequoyah intended to remain in the west, Chief Pathkiller instructed John Ross to forward it to him with a proper letter of transmission, which he did. Sequoyah wore the medal through life and it was buried with him.

The first Cherokee type was cast in Boston under the supervision of Reverend Samuel A. Worcester, and in the December number, 1827, of the Missionary Herald, appeared the first to the fifth verses of the first chapter of Genesis in Cherokee, which was the first printing done in the Sequoian characters.

The Cherokee Nation Council provided for their first printing office by the following resolution:

"New Echota, Cherokee Nation, November 2nd, 1826.

"Resolved by the National Committee and Council. That a house shall be built for a printing office of the following dimensions: 24x20 feet, one story high, shingle roof, with one fireplace, one door in the end of the house, one floor and a window in each side of the house two lights deep and ten feet long, to be chinked and lined on the inside with narrow plank, with the necessary watering benches and type desks requisite for a printing office.

George Lowrey, President pro-tem (of the
Committee),
Major Ridge, Speaker (of the Council),
his
Path x Killer, (Principal Chief),
mark
Ch. R. Hicks, (Assistant Chief).
Alexander McCoy, Clerk Committee,
Elias Boudinot, Clerk Council."*

The Council, apparently not anticipating an early installation of
the printing establishment, two days later, passed this resolution:

"New Echota, Cherokee Nation, November 4th, 1826.

"Resolved by the National Committee and Council, That David
Brown and George Lowrey be, and they are hereby appointed to translate
eight copies of the laws of the Cherokee Nation, as early as convenient,
into the Cherokee language, written in characters invented by George
Guess, and also to translate one copy of the New Testament in the same
characters and to present them to the General Council when completed
and the National Committee and Council shall compensate them for their
services.

John Ross, President National Committee.
Major Ridge, Speaker.
his
Approved—Path x Killer
mark
Ch. R. Hicks.
A. McCoy, Clerk of Committee,
E. Boudinott, Clerk Council."†

Active preparations looking forward to the early publication of
the national paper was a part of the work of the council of 1827, as is
evinced by these two resolutions, one of which was not dated.

"Resolved by the Nation Committee and Council, That a person
be appointed whose duty it shall be to edit a weekly newspaper at New

---

* Laws of the Cherokee Nation, 1852, page 81.
† Laws of the Cherokee Nation, 1852, page 81.

Echota, to be entitled, THE CHEROKEE PHOENIX, and also to translate matter in the Cherokee language for the columns of said paper as well as to translate all public documents which may be submitted for publication, and the sum of three hundred dollars per annum be allowed said editor and translator for his services.

"New Echota, October 18th, 1827.[*]

        Elijah Hicks, President Nation'l Committee,
        Major Ridge, Speaker Council.
Approved—Wm. Hicks
        Jno Ross.
A. McCoy, Clerk Committee,
E. Boudinott, Clerk National Council.

"Resolved by the National Committee and Council, That Isaac N. Harris be, and he is hereby appointed principal Printer for the Cherokee Nation, whose salary shall be four hundred dollars a year, and whose duties shall be to attend to the printing of the paper to be printed at New Echota, and it shall further be the duty of said Harris to employ, and he is hereby authorized to employ a journeyman printer, of sober and studious habits in behalf of the Cherokee Nation, in order that the aforesaid paper may be successfully carried into effect.

"And be it further resolved, That the salary of the journeyman printer so employed, shall be three hundred dollars a year.

"And be it further resolved, That the commencement of the salaries of said printers shall commence and begin on the day of the commencement of the paper, which shall take place now as soon as practicable, and that the aforesaid respective sums be, and they are hereby appropriated out of any monies in the Treasury not otherwise appropriated, and it shall be the duty of the Editor at the expiration of a term to certify that the printers have well and faithfully performed their contracts as printers, which certificates shall be presented to the National Treasurer for payment, who is hereby authorized to engage the aforesaid in an obligation for sufficient penalty for default for the certain performance of printing the National paper.

---

[*] Laws of the Cherokee Nation, 1852, page 85. In the original volume a typographical error made the year 1826 instead of 1827.

Elijah Hicks, President N. Committee,
Major Ridge, Speaker.
Approved—Wm. Hicks,
John Ross.
A. McCoy, Clerk Committee,
E. Boudinott, Clerk N. Council."[*]

The printers arrived at New Echota on December 23rd, 1827, and at once commenced to study the Cherokee syllabary, but before the press arrived, which was in the latter part of January, 1828, Harris had given up the task of learning the syllabary and the task of setting the Cherokee type fell upon his assistant, John F. Wheeler, and later John W. Candy, a quarter blood Cherokee.

The press had been purchased in Boston, and the paper in Knoxville, Tennessee. New windows had to be made in the office, as the first ones had been so placed that they would be beneath the cases, and for that reason would not give the necessary light.

Sequoyah's arrangement of the letters of his syllabary had not been made in accordance with any phonetic system, and for that reason Reverend Worcester rearranged them in phonetic order. Stands and cases had to be made for the type, and on account of the fact that the syllabary contained eighty-six characters, it became necessary to make cases having over one hundred boxes; so as to hold the necessary letters, spaces and punctuations. The press was inked with balls made of deer skin and stuffed with wool.[†]

Volume 1, Number 1, of the Cherokee Phoenix was issued from the press on February 21, 1828. The last issue was that of May 31, 1834. No. 52 of Vol. 5.[‡]

The following amendatory resolution was adopted by the Cherokee Council:

"Resolved by the National Committee and Council, That the salaries of the persons attached to the Cherokee Phoenix shall be paid quarterly. This to be an amendment to the resolution providing for their salaries, dated Oct. 18, 1827.

"Be it further Resolved, That, in order to provide against

---

[*] Laws of the Cherokee Nation, 1852, page 84.
[†] Bibliography of the Iroquoian Language, by James Constantine Pilling, Washington, 1888, page 41.
[‡] Ibid.

inconvenience that may arise for want of paper, ink, or other articles requisite in the printing department, it shall be the duty of the Editor to provide from time to time the necessary articles as may be needed, which shall be defrayed out of the proceeds of the Cherokee Phoenix.

"Be it further Resolved, That the Editor of the Phoenix be, and he is hereby, required to enter into bond with sufficient security for the faithful performance of all his duties; and that said Editor be and is hereby authorized to receive all monies that may arise from subscriptions for the Phoenix, or from the publication of any other matter; he is also expressly empowered to use his discretion in every respect, in order that the Nation may be benefitted[sic] by the institution. All monies arising from the Phoenix shall be paid into the Treasury of the Cherokee Nation quarterly.

"Be it further Resolved, That in case of the sickness of the Editor, death or resignation, the Principal Chief shall have the power of appointing a suitable Editor to take charge of the paper in the editorial department, whose salary shall be the same as his predecessor's.

"Be it further Resolved, That in case of sickness, death or resignation of the printers, the place or places so vacated shall be filled by the principal chief. The salaries shall be the same as the former printers. And in order to have a native printer, it shall be the duty of the Editor to procure, if possible a Cherokee apprentice, whose clothes and board shall be paid out of the proceeds of the Cherokee Phoenix. The clothing of the apprentices shall be common and comfortable. It shall be the duty of the Editor to engage, and make arrangements for said apprentice's board. In the selection of the apprentice, the Editor is required to choose one who speaks and writes the same dialect* with the inventor of the Cherokee alphabet.

New Echota, 19th October, 1828.

Elijah Hicks, President N. Committee.

Major Ridge, Speaker.

Approved—William Hicks.

Jno. Ross.

A. McCoy, Clerk of Committee.

E. Boudinot, Clerk N. Council."‡

---

* Underhill.
‡ Laws of the Cherokee Nation, 1852, page 85.

Miss Janana Ballard. Cherokee Genealogy No. 111—$1^1 1^2 10^3 5^4 2^5 2^6 1^7$.
Graduated from the Cherokee National Female Seminary on June 26,
1896.

On May 8, 1828, Sequoyah was one of the signers of the treaty between the United States and the "Western" Cherokees, at Washington, D. C. It was during this visit that he sat for the painter, Charles B. King. He signed the "Act of Union" between the Eastern and Western Cherokees, on July 12, 1839, as "President of the Western Cherokees"[†] and on the following 6th of September he was one of the signers of the Cherokee Constitution.

In the spring of 1842, after having cautioned all of his associates to keep their destination as secret as possible, Sequoyah, accompanied by eight other Cherokees, as follows: His son Teesee Guess, Worm, John Elijah, Oo-wo-si-ti, Cah-ta-ta, Nu-wo-ta-na, Tallatoo and Coteska, started to the southwest in an attempt to find a Cherokee settlement that was said to be located in the vicinity of the Rio Grande River.

Worm, who was well acquainted among the southwestern tribes and spoke several of their languages, acted as interpreter and guide. Coteska was only a youth. Besides the horses that they rode they had three pack horses.

Sequoyah's company started, and after stopping one night with Archibald Campbell at Park Hill, they proceeded westward, crossing Arkansas River below Fort Gibson. They traversed the Muskogee and Choctaw Nations, and in the latter they visited Key's Town, a Cherokee settlement on Blue River, and then crossed Red River at the mouth of Cache Creek.

After crossing Red River, Sequoyah and the others stopped and sent Worm ahead to look out a suitable route and to see if he could find out whether there were any Cherokees at any of the towns or camps that could guide them directly to the southwestern Cherokee settlement.

Worm was absent for twelve days on this trip, and while at a Wichita village he purchased three bushels of corn, for which he had to pay nine dollars.

Upon the return of Worm, the party proceeded to the Wichita town, where they received hospitable treatment. From this town, Sequoyah sent all of his companions back home, except his son Teesee and Worm. After a few days' stop here, they resumed their journey

---

[†] The title of "President of the Western Cherokees" was an unauthorized and fictitious title created for this special occasion by the parties to this "agreement." This "agreement" was made for the purpose of making it one of the basis of appeal to the authorities at Washington and to the citizens of the eastern states.

southward. While they were in the vicinity of San Antonio they had all of their horses stolen by a band of Tawakony Indians.

After having traveled for some distance to the southwest on foot, Teesee and Worm, at the suggestion of Sequoyah, left him in a cave near the Mau-luke River, after having provided him with twenty days' rations. In this cave was a higher ledge of rock and the younger men leaned a tree trunk against it so that in case the stream rose and got into the cave that Sequoyah might use the tree trunk to aid him in getting to the higher ledge. Sequoyah, during his journey, used all the available time possible in writing, but it is not certain as to what this work related.

Teesee and Worm then proceeded to reconnoiter and after several days they came to a Mexican adobe town in which they noted that the houses all had flat roofs. They stayed at this town two days and then proceeded to San Cranto, at which place they met Standing Rock, a Cherokee from the town for which they were searching.

Standing Rock guided them to the Cherokee town, which was ten miles from the Mexican village, and then they returned to the cave in which they had left Sequoyah, but on arriving there they found that the water had swept through the cave and that Sequoyah had disappeared, and upon their making a circuit around the camp they found the tracks of a man, which was easily identified as those of Sequoyah, on account of the fact that he was lame. They also found a letter that had been written four days before, in which he said that the water had washed away all of his provisions and that he had started in an attempt to trail them. They tracked him to the Mau-luke River, which he had crossed on a raft, and a short distance from the river they found where a fire had been recently kindled, and from this place, while they found the tracks of several persona and horses, they were not able to track the aged Sequoyah any further.

They then hurried on as fast as they could in the trail that the horses had taken and on the evening of the second day they came to a dense thicket into which the horse tracks led. They followed the tracks and soon came upon Sequoyah, who was sitting by a camp fire enjoying his evening meal, and a horse was lariated near by.

Sequoyah told them that the water rose in the cave on the twelfth day after their departure and washed away all of his possessions except the clothing that he had on, a blanket and a steel.[*] He used the tree trunk and climbed upon the ledge; he being afraid that the water would reach him there, made his way to a small hill top, where he wrapped his blanket around him and laid down to rest as well as he could, although it was still raining. The next morning he built a fire and dried out his clothes and blanket.

He then returned to the cave and upon searching the banks of the stream below his camp found most of his papers and a few other articles. He then wrote the letter and tacked it on a tree and started out on the trail that they had taken, hoping to meet them on their return. After crossing the river he ascended a small ridge to see if he could see anything of them, and just as he came to the top of the ridge he met a number of strange Indians, who, through sign language, he ascertained to be Delawares, and he in the same way informed them that he was a Cherokee and of the circumstances by which he was there, alone.

They build a fire and had a meal together, and after this meal they asked Sequoyah to accompany them back to their camps, which were to the northward. They were most probably buffalo hunters or possibly traders. Sequoyah made them understand that he could not accompany them, but that he had to go ahead and meet his party, and asked them to go with him. They signed that they could not go with him but that on account of his age and infirmity they would give him a horse and some provisions. They then accompanied him to the place at which he was then camped, and they, taking leave, turned to the north.

By their accounts this was the eighteenth day after they had left him in the cave.

They then retraced their way to the Cherokee town. About three miles before they reached this town they came to a Negro settlement at which they found two or three Negroes that spoke the Cherokee language, probably runaways.

After staying at the Cherokee town a few days, Worm returned to the Cherokee Nation.

During the fall of 1843 reports reached the Cherokee Nation that Sequoyah had died some time previous, but this was not definitely confirmed for some time. The information had become so definite by

---

[*] The "steel" was a flat piece of steel that was used to strike a piece of flint rock in such a way that sparks would be made to fly and ignite material that was held to catch it. The back of the blade of a pocket knife would have served for the same purpose.

Joel Bryan Mayes. Cherokee genealogy No. $1^1 1^2 2^3 3^4 5^5$.
Graduated from the Cherokee National Male Seminary in
February, 1855. Principal Chief of the Cherokee Nation
from January, 1888, to December 4, 1891.

January, 1845, that T. Hartley Crawford, the United States Commissioner of Indian Affairs, offered on the seventeenth of that month a reward of two hundred dollars for the recovery of Sequoyah's body. The reward was never claimed.

The following letter gives the most circumstantial account of the death of Sequoyah:

"Warrens Trading House,
"Red River, Apl 21st, 1845.

"We, the undersigned Cherokees, direct from the Spanish Dominions, do hereby certify that George Guess, of the Cherokee Nation, Arkansas, departed this life in the town of San-fernando in the month of August, 1843, and his son Chusaleta is at this time on the Brasos River, Texas, about thirty miles above the falls, and he intends returning home this fall.

"Given under our hands the day and date written.

his
Standing x Rock.
mark.
his
Standing x Bowles.
mark.
his
Watch x Justice.
mark.

Witnesses: Daniel G. Watson, Jesse Chisholm."*

The main sources of information, heretofore accessible to the general public, relating to Sequoyah, has been the sketch of Sequoyah in McKinney and Hall's Indian Tribes, Volume 1, 1856; the article in the September, 1870, issue of Harper's Monthly Magazine, by William A. Phillipe[sic], and "Sequoyah, the Cherokee Cadmus," by George E. Foster of Milford, New Hampshire, published in 1885.

The McKinney and Hall sketch is quite accurate. The article by Colonel William A. Phillips is made up generally from statements made to him by different parties several years after the death of Sequoyah, and on account of his vivid imagination many of his other statements are a

* All of the circumstances of the journey and death of Sequoyah, except the above given certificate, is from the statement of Worm, as given in the Cherokee Advocate, Volume I. No, 40, published June 26th, 1845.

unreliable as that in which he says that one of Sequoyah's sons was a soldier in his regiment.

The statement of Sequoyah's descent as I give it is from the account of Mrs. Catherine Downing, the daughter of Teesee Guess and the granddaughter of Sequoyah. Mrs. Downing, who is still alive, is a very intelligent woman.

The verbose and fanciful volume on Sequoyah by George E. Foster was prepared after a hurried trip to the Indian Territory in the early eighties of the nineteenth century, some forty years after the death of Sequoyah, and reference to foreign bibliographic material.

It is regrettable that such works have of necessity been the sole reference of Sequoyah, when Worm's account in the Cherokee Advocate, together with the contemporaneous accounts of Boudinot, bear on their faces the imprint of reliability.

Not being certain of the death of Sequoyah, the Cherokee National Council enacted:

"An Act for the benefit of George Guess.

"Be it enacted by the National Council, That in lieu of the sum allowed to George Guess, in consideration of his invention of the Cherokee Alphabet, passed December 10th, 1841,[*] and which is hereby repealed, the sum of three hundred dollars be paid to the said George Guess out of the National Treasury annually during his natural life.

"Sec. 2d. Be it further enacted, That in case of the death of George Guess, that the same shall be paid to his wife, Mrs. Sally Guess, annually, during her natural life.

"Tahlequah, Dec. 29th, 1843.

"Approved—John Ross."[†]

The act for paying the annual pension to Sequoyah or to his widow, in case of his death, for the year 1844, was as follows:

"An Act appropriating three hundred dollars to George Guess for the year 1844.

"Be is enacted by the National Council, That the sum of three hundred dollars be, and the same is hereby appropriated, out of any money in the Treasury not otherwise appropriated, for the benefit of George Guess, or his wife Sarah, for the year 1844.

---

[*] The act of December 10th, 1841, here referred to cannot be found.

[†] Laws of the Cherokee Nation, 1852, page 116.

"Tahlequah, December 24th, 1844.

"Approved—John Ross."[‡]

On November 4th, 1851, the Cherokee National Council changed the name of Skin Bayou District,[§] which at that time was one of the eight political divisions of the Cherokee Nation, to Sequoyah District, as this was the district in which he had lived. The act changing the name was as follows:

"An Act changing the name of Skin Bayou District.

"Be it enacted by the National Council, that the name of Skin Bayou District be, and the same is hereby changed, and that the said district shall be called from and after the passage of this act, Sequoyah; and so much of the act passed November 4th, 1840, as militates against this act be and the same is hereby repealed.

"Tahlequah, November 4th, 1851.

"Approved—John Ross."[‖]

The National Council, by an act of October 25th, 1843, authorized the publication of National paper at Tahlequah, which was to be known as the Cherokee Advocate. The editor was to be elected by the National Council; this office was first filled by William Potter Ross, a nephew of Chief John Ross. Young Ross had recently graduated from Princeton University and was a scholarly and courtly gentleman.

The first issue of the Cherokee Advocate appeared on September 26th, 1844, and was continued until September 28th, 1853.

The Advocate was discontinued until after the Civil War, and Volume 2, No. 2 of the second series was issued April 26th, 1870, and the last known issue of this series was December 26th, 1874, shortly after which time the office and all the fixtures were destroyed by an accidental fire.

Volume 1, No. 1, of the third series was issued on March 4th, 1876.

Missions and Missionaries.

In 1801 James Vann, a wealthy half-blood Cherokee-Scotchman, had a commodious two-story brick dwelling on Chicamauga Creek in

---

[‡] Laws of the Cherokee Nation, 1852, page 116.

[§] Skin Bayou District was name for Skin Bayou Creek.

[‖] Laws of the Cherokee Nation, 1852, page 227.

North Georgia, and in April of this year Reverends Abraham Steiner and Cottleib Byhan, Moravian missionaries, became his invited guests until they could erect the initial mission buildings at Spring Place, so named on account of the number of springs in the vicinity. From that time for nearly a hundred years the earnest and zealous Moravian missionaries labored among the Cherokees.

In 1803 Reverend Gideon Blackburn, a Presbyterian, opened two schools among the Cherokees in the vicinity of the present Tennessee-North Carolina line.

He made two trips through the Cherokee country. One of six weeks in 1808 and one of twelve weeks during the succeeding year. Besides acquainting himself with the conditions of the country, he encouraged various industries; especially that of preparing and spinning cotton and wool. This bore rich fruits, in a few years, in the abundance of cloth that was woven and worn by the Cherokees. This cloth became so popular among them that the buckskin garment was a rare sight in the Cherokee Nation by 1830, and the striped homemade hunting shirt (a loose frock coat, trimmed with red yarn fringe) of the Cherokee became as distinctive a mark as was the Scotch tartan.

After the Cherokees came West and became the peacemakers of the plains, this Cherokee hunting shirt became the safest guarantee of life of any emblem that might be exhibited to the hostile Indians between the Mississippi River and Rocky Mountains.

On account of ill health, Reverend Blackburn gave up his missionary work among the Cherokees in 1810.

Mr. Richards Keys (VII, $1^1,4^2,9^2$) told me that he and a companion were hunting on Caney River, in what is now the southern part of Washington County, Oklahoma, in the early fifties and while away from their camp they had some of their horses stolen, leaving them with only the saddle horses that they had been riding. They started out to search for their horses and had not gone very far, and while riding through a swamp that was covered with high grass, they saw a band of mounted, blanketed Pawnees. This location was at that time miles from any Cherokee habitation and the Pawnees commenced at once to gallop around them in an ever narrowing circle. The Pawnees threw themselves on the sides of their horses opposite the now thoroughly frightened young men, and only one foot over the horse's back could be discerned. Keys and his friend were Cherokees, but like most other Cherokees, they could not be distinguished from their white neighbors. The Pawnees evidently thought that they could kill and rob the lone white men and no one would know who did it, as they themselves lived many miles westward and were only here on a temporary hunt. Keys said he expected every moment to be a target for either an arrow or a bullet, when he saw his comrade make a sudden downward movement with his left hand, which he had been holding high above his head, and at once each blanket Indian sat erect on his horse, with an arrow or gun directed at them, but the action of his comrade was quicker than were the Pawnees, for he grasped the lapel of his overcoat and tearing it open he revealed his Cherokee hunting shirt underneath. The Pawnees at once lowered their guns and bows, and riding up to Keys and his companion, saluted them with "Nowa, Cherokees." They helped Keys and his friend to find their horses and parted in friendship.

THE A. B. C. F. M.

The American Board of Commissioners for Foreign Missions commenced their beneficent work among the Cherokees in 1817, continuing until 1861.

Their stations were established in the following places and years, consecutively:

1817—Brainard.
1819—Taloney, afterward called Carmel.
1820—Creek Path.
1823—Will's Town.
1823—Turnip Mountain, afterward called Hawais.
1824—Candy's Creek.
1830—New Echota.
1820—Dwight (in Pope County, Arkansas).
1828—Mulberry (in Pope County, Arkansas).
1826—Union, taken over by the amalgamation with the United Foreign Society (in Mayes County, Oklahoma).
1829—Park Hill (in Cherokee County, Oklahoma).
1828—Dwight (in Sequoyah County, Oklahoma), moved from Pope County, Arkansas.
1828—Fairfield (in Adair County, Oklahoma), moved from Pope County, Arkansas, where it had been known as Mulberry.

1829—"The Mission at the Forks of the Illinois" (in Cherokee County, Oklahoma).

MORAVIAN MISSIONS.

The missions of the United Brethren were established in the following years at the places indicated:

1803—Spring Place (in Georgia).

1821—Oothcalogy (in Georgia), thirty miles south of Spring Place, was established by Reverend John Gambold.

A mission on Barren Fork, below the mouth of Tyner's Creek (in Adair County, Oklahoma), was moved to Harmony on Beatty's Prairie (in Delaware County, Oklahoma) and later to Spring Place, on the west side of Illinois River, in the northern part of what is now Cherokee County, Oklahoma.

Honey Creek Mission (in Delaware County, Oklahoma) was taken over from the Presbyterians at the death of Reverend John Huss, a full blood Cherokee Presbyterian minister, who had maintained this mission.

BAPTIST MISSIONS AND MISSIONARIES.

Reverend Humphrey Posey, a native of North Carolina, was appointed by the Baptist Board as a missionary to the Cherokees on October 13, 1817[*]. He immediately repaired to the western part of his own state, where there were living at that time several thousand of this tribe. Having established a few schools, he felt called to do some exploring in the regions west of the Mississippi, doubtless with a view of locating his work there. His protracted, absence caused a loss of interest in the schools, also a necessary suspension of them. On his return, early in 1820, he established a missionary station at Valley Town, on Hiwassee River, in the southwest corner of the state. Mr. Thomas Dawson was appointed assistant. A farm of eighty acres was cleared and put in cultivation and three houses built. Shortly after the school started it had forty pupils.[†]

Evan Jones was born in Brecknockshire, Wales, on May 14, 1788. At the age of fifteen he was apprenticed to a linen draper and

---

[*] Walter N. Wyeth, in Poor Lo, Philadelphia, Pa., 1896, page 20.

[†] Wyeth, page 21.

spent a number of years with him. While there he met Miss Elizabeth Lanigan, who was also working in this store, and in course of time she became his wife.

The Joneses emigrated to America, reaching Philadelphia early in 1821, and subsequently settled in the village of Berwyn, Pennsylvania. Mr. Jones had previously left the formal Church of England and joined the Methodists, but during the summer of 1821 he and his wife became members of the "Great Valley Baptist Church," near their home. It was under the pastorage of Reverend Thomas Roberts, who, with others, was at this time preparing to enter upon a mission to the Cherokees.

A month after the reception of Mr. and Mrs. Jones into the Baptist Church found them members of the missionary band to the Cherokees.[*] Traveling in four wagons, these missionaries arrived at Valley Town, in the Cherokee country (now western North Carolina), in September, 1821. Reverend Roberts took the directing office of missionary superintendent and among the other assignments were Mr. Isaac Cleaver, blacksmith; Mr. John Farrier, farmer and weaver; Mr. Jones, teacher, and it is not known what the other score of people did.

Notley and Tinsawatee.

A mission was established at Notley, sixteen miles southwest of Valley Town, in the summer of 1822. Shortly afterwards another mission was established at Tinsawatee,[**] sixty miles southwest from Valley Town, in Georgia.[†] In 1823 the Baptist missionaries received their first convert, in the person of John Timson.[‡] In this year they were joined by Reverend and Mrs. Duncan O'Bryant, who were assigned to the station at Tinsawatee.

The date of the ordination of Evan Jones to the ministry is not known, but we do know that by 1825 he and his family were the only ones of the Great Valley missionary band that still remained with the Cherokee mission work.

Reverend O'Bryant moved the mission from Tinsawatee to

---

[*] Wyeth, page 49.
[**] The translation of Tinsawatee is Old Tennessee Town.
[†] Wyeth, page 21.
[‡] Wyeth, page 59.

Hickory Log, a distance of some ten miles.[§]

Kaneeda, a full blood Cherokee, was converted at Hiwassee in 1829 and became the first native Baptist minister among the Cherokees. On account of his character, Reverend Jones gave him the English name of John Wickliffe. He began preaching in 1831 and was ordained in 1833. He died in Saline District, Cherokee Nation (now Mayes County, Oklahoma), on November 22, 1857.[*]

During the time that these Baptist missionaries were prosecuting their work among the full bloods in the eastern part of the Cherokee Nation, Jesse Bushyhead, the son of a prominent half blood family, after having attended school in Tennessee, joined the Baptist Church and was baptized in 1830. He returned to the Cherokee Nation and gathered together a congregation at Ahmohee, which was in his immediate neighborhood. It was not until quite a while after he had built up a good church here that he met any of the Baptist missionaries.[†] He was ordained to the ministry in 1833, at the same time as was John Wickliffe. Reverend Bushyhead had a circuit of two hundred and forty miles, in which he was assisted from 1834 to 1838 by Reverend Bear Carrier, a young Cherokee minister.

Reverend Bushyhead was one of the leaders of the Ross party, serving in many public offices, being at the time of his death[‡] Chief Justice of the Cherokee Nation. His disinterestedness in the feudal and political troubles among his people gained for him the peculiar distinction of being the only man of any consequence among the Cherokees who habitually traveled among his people in the troublous period of 1839-46, unarmed, except, as he said, with his Bible.

He was one of the captains of detachments of the emigrant Cherokees. His detachment started on October 5, 1838; was delayed at the Mississippi River for one month on account of ice and after having traveled through Southern Missouri they reached the Cherokee Nation "West" on February 23, 1839. Eighty-two of his company died en route.

Oganoyah, a full blood Cherokee, was a contemporary Baptist minister with Bushyhead and Wickliffe.

[§] Wyeth, page 38.
[*] Wyeth, page 39.
[†] Wyeth, page 61.
[‡] Rev. Jesse Bushyhead died on July 17, 1844.

The Baptist Church membership in 1835 in the Cherokee Nation "East" was two hundred and twenty-seven.

Mrs. Elizabeth Lanigan Jones died at Valley Town on February 5, 1831.[*] Rev. Jones' second wife was Miss Pauline Cunningham.

About thirty families from the vicinity of Hickory Log Mission, under Reverend O'Bryant, migrated to the Cherokee Nation "West" in 1831, establishing New Hope Mission, on Barren Fork Creek (in what is now Adair County, Oklahoma), about two miles from the Arkansas line. They shortly afterwards added a grist and sawmill.

Reverend O'Bryant died in 1834 and was succeeded by Reverend Samuel Aldrich of Cincinnati, Ohio, who died after one year of service. This mission then lapsed.[†]

Other accessions to the missionary working force among the Eastern Cherokees were Leonard and Mrs. Butterfield and Miss Sarah Rayner in 1832 and Chandler Curtis in 1835.

Reverend Bushyhead established a camp near the Arkansas line upon his arrival in 1839, at which rations were issued to needy emigrants and for this reason the camp was locally known as "Bread Town,"[‡] but Mr. Bushyhead immediately commenced his religious work here and the location soon became known as "Baptist Mission," the name that it justly bears to this day, although the mission was removed to Tahlequah by John B. Jones, in 1867. The Joneses settled at and became a part of Baptist Mission on their arrival in the Cherokee Nation "West."

David McNair Foreman and Lewis Downing were added to the list of strong native Baptist ministers among the Cherokees in the decades of 1839-59.

John Buttrick Jones, son of Reverend Evan and Mrs. Elizabeth Lanigan Jones, was born at Valley Town, North Carolina, on December 24, 1824. He was Cherokee interpreter for his father at the age of thirteen. Was baptized by Reverend John Wickliffe in 1844. The Joneses, assisted by Hervey Upham and Mark Tiger, published at Baptist

---

[*] Wyeth, page 54.
[†] Wyeth, page 38.
[‡] "Bread Town" or Baptist Mission was in what is now section 13, township 18 north, range 25 east, in the State of Oklahoma.

Colonel Johnson Harris. Cherokee genealogy No. XI—
$1^1 3^2 5^3 11^4$. Principal Chief of the Cherokee Nation from
December 23, 1891, to November, 1895.

Mission the Cherokee Messenger, a monthly missionary publication, a part of which was printed in the Cherokee language. Its first issue was in August, 1844. Only about fourteen issues were printed.

John B. Jones graduated from the University of Rochester, New York, in 1855. He was ordained to the ministry in that city on July 14, 1855, and was married there in October of the same year to Miss Jennie M. Smith. They repaired immediately to Baptist Mission, Cherokee Nation, and entered the missionary work.[§]

Both Evan Jones and his son, John B. Jones, were men of magnetic and sympathetic presences, splendid acquisitive minds and rare executive abilities.

While the father was perfectly conversant with the Cherokee language, he always used an interpreter when preaching to the Cherokees. The son, having been born in the Cherokee country, rapidly gained a facile and perfect knowledge of the Cherokee language and customs and no man or men were ever able to sway the minds and policies of the full blood Cherokees as did this father and son.

They were the real dictators of the Cherokee Nation from 1839 to 1867, through the numerically dominant full bloods, who as a body were always swayed by impulse rather than reason. As ministers of the gospel they were apparently meek and humble, but the sentiments that they powerfully and insidiously engendered among the full bloods were perforce the governmental policies of Chief Ross.

At the same time they almost always courted the good will of the astute and suave Ross, but upon the accession of his nephew, William P. Ross, to the chieftaincy, they broke with him and by promoting an alliance, in 1867, between the friends of Lieutenant Colonel, the Reverend Lewis Downing, and the ex-Confederate Cherokees, they formed the Downing party, which after this time elected all of the chiefs except one.[*]

With hardly a break the Baptist educational succession has been: Valley Town Mission, 1820-39; Baptist Mission, 1839-67; Baptist Mission at Tahlequah, 1867-85, and Bacone University at Muskogee, Indian Territory 1835—.

[§] Wyeth, page 55.
[*] Dennis W. Bushyhead was elected in 1879 by the newly formed National party and was re-elected in 1883.

Chief Charles Thompson (Oochalata[†]), who spoke the Cherokee language only, and was always accounted a full blood Cherokee,[‡] although his mother was a white woman who could not talk English, was ordained as a Baptist minister while he was chief. Although he had been preaching for several years he had been denied ordination because he was a lawyer.[§]

Reverend Evan Jones died in August, 1873, and Reverend John Buttrick Jones died on June 13, 1876.

PRESBYTERIAN MISSIONS AND MISSIONARIES.

In 1816 Reverend Cyrus Kingsbury, a native of Alstead, New Hampshire, visited the Cherokee country, with a view of locating a mission among this tribe. He reported favorably on the proposition and was delegated by the American Board of Commissioners for Foreign Missions, a non-denominational organization, composed of Presbyterians and Congregationalists, to erect the necessary buildings. He arrived at the proposed site, on Chicamauga Creek, on January 13, 1817, and immediately commenced the establishment of Brainard Mission, which was destined to be the precursor of much missionary work among the Cherokees. Brainard is seven miles east of the present city of Chattanooga, Tennessee, and two miles from the Georgia line.

On March 7, 1817, Moody Hall, a native of Cornish, New Hampshire, and Loring S. Williams, a native of Pownal, Vermont, arrived at Brainard.

Reverend Ard Hoyt, a native of Danbury, Connecticut, and Reverend Daniel Sabin Buttrick, a native of Andover, Massachusetts, with their families, arrived at Brainard on January 3, 1818.

On March 10, 1818, Reverend William Chamberlin, a native of Newbury, Vermont, arrived at Brainard. He was the affianced husband

---

[†] Oochalata had only this Cherokee name until after his election to the Cherokee senate from Delaware District on August 5, 1867, after which date he thought that it might be well to have an English name also. He said that Dr. Jeter Lynch Thompson had been senator from that district for many years and for that reason he would call himself Thompson, retaining the Chala or Charles from his Cherokee name Oo-chala-ta.

[‡] All Cherokees who spoke the Cherokee language preferably were locally known as full bloods.

[§] Wyeth, page 62.

of Miss Flora, the daughter of Reverend and Mrs. Hoyt, and they were married at the mission on March 22, 1818.

In January, 1818, Catherine Brown, aged 17, a three-quarters blood Cherokee girl, joined the Presbyterian Church at Brainard. The mission among the Cherokees being in successful operation, Reverends Kingsbury and Williams left the Cherokee mission work for a new field among the Choctaws, on or about the first of June, 1818.

In 1819 Reverend Ard Hoyt was superintendent of Brainard, with Reverend Daniel S. Buttrick as assistant. The school had sixty pupils this year. One of them, Lydia Lowry, aged sixteen, joined the Presbyterian Church and was baptized on January 31, 1819. She was afterwards the author of the first Cherokee hymn.

President James Monroe, accompanied by Major General Edmund P. and Mrs. Gaines, visited Brainard on May 27 and 28, 1819, stopping over night there.

John Arch, "an unpromising looking young man," entered the school this year. He was a full blood Cherokee from western North Carolina. He soon became a good English scholar and interpreter and was noted for his sincere Christianity and splendid character. He died at Brainard June 18, 1825.

Reverend William Potter and Dr. Elizur Butler, with their families, arrived at Brainard January 10, 1821.

John C. Ellsworth arrived at Brainard on November 24, 1821, and on the succeeding nineteenth of December John Vail and Henry Parker arrived.

A grist mill, a sawmill and a blacksmith shop were installed at Brainard in 1821. These were for the use of the mission and to accommodate the public.

At the end of this year there were eighty-seven Cherokee pupils in attendance at Brainard—thirty girls and fifty-seven boys.

Mr. Dean, a blacksmith from Vermont, with his wife, arrived in January, 1822, and two months later Ainsworth E. Blunt, a cooper, and Sylvester Ellis, a farmer, arrived. The former was a native of New Hampshire and the latter of Vermont.

In May, 1822, the property of the mission was valued at $17,390 and there were eighty Cherokee and two Osage pupils. These Osages, John Osage Ross and Lydia James, had been adopted by the Cherokees after they had killed their parents in a fight at Claremore Mound, in the

67

present county of Rogers, state of Oklahoma, in Anoya or Strawberry Moon of 1818.

On October 12, 1822, Mr. and Mrs. Isaac Proctor of New Hampshire arrived at Brainard and on the thirteenth of the same month Mr. Frederick Ellsworth of Vermont arrived.

In 1823 Reverend Ard Hoyt was missionary; Dr. Elizur Butler, physician; Sylvester Ellis, schoolmaster; John Vail, Henry Parker and Frederick Ellsworth, farmers; Erastus Bean and Ainsworth E. Blunt, mechanics.

In 1824 the following were attached to Brainard: Reverend William Potter, Reverend Daniel S. Buttrick; John C. Ellsworth, boys' instructor; Miss Sophia Sawyer, girls' instructor; Henry Parker, Ainsworth E. Blunt and Jonah Hemingway, farmers and mechanics, and Dean, the blacksmith.

Reverend Samuel Austin Worcester, a native of Peacham, Vermont, arrived at Brainard on October 21, 1825.

In 1826 Reverend S. A. Worcester was missionary at Brainard; John C. Ellsworth, teacher; Henry Parker, John Vail and Jonah Hemingway, farmers; Ainsworth E. Blunt, farmer and mechanic, and Miss Sophia Sawyer, teacher.

The census of the Cherokee Nation "East" for the year of 1824 showed 14,283 Cherokee citizens. They owned at this time 1,277 negro slaves. There were 18 schools in the nation, with an attendance of 314 scholars of both sexes. They had 36 grist mills, 13 sawmills, 762 looms, 2,486 spinning wheels, 172 wagons, 2,923 plows, 7,683 horses, 22,531 cattle, 46,732 swine, 2,566 sheep, 430 goats, 62 blacksmith shops, 9 stores, two tan yards and one powder mill.[*]

"In one district there was about a thousand good books and eleven periodicals, both religious and political. They were subscribed for and read at this time (1826). Most of the schools were under the care and tuition of Christian missionaries."[†] The Western Cherokees were even more prosperous than were their Eastern brethren.

Miss Lucy Ames, a native of Groton, Massachusetts, arrived at Brainard on November 7, 1827.

---

[*] Address of Edward Everett, representative from Massachusetts, delivered in the House of Representatives on May 19, 1830.
[†] Mss., Chamberlin.

In 1828 there were fifty pupils at Brainard.

In 1829 Miss Ames was teaching at Brainard.

"The station at Brainard sustained a great loss by the burning of the principal portion of the mission buildings on the twelfth of March, 1830, including the kitchen, dining hall, school rooms for both departments, lodging rooms for both scholars and family, together with supplies and furniture. The fire was so rapid that not more than fifteen minutes were allowed for awakening and saving the occupants. There were more than fifty children, besides the mission family.

"The missionaries, almost frantic with the responsibility, rushed into and through the burning buildings, almost into the very jaws of death, to see if any of the beloved charge remained unsaved. Then, when the roof had fallen in, a rush was made down to the bank of the beautiful Chickamauga, where the saved ones had been ordered to go. There in the gray morning twilight the lines are formed, the count is made and all drop on their knees to thank God for deliverance. All were saved."[*]

Carmel Mission.

A mission was established by Reverend Moody Hall on the Federal Road, in Georgia, sixty miles southeast of Brainard, on November 2, 1819."[†]

Carmel was at first known as Taloney.[§] The school was opened in May, 1820, and by September of the next year there were thirty pupils attending.[‡]

Reverend and Mrs. John Thompson and Miss Catherine Fuller were attached to the mission on January 23, 1822, and in the next year Reverend Daniel S. Buttrick was attached as missionary.

Carmel belonged to a Georgia Presbytery, and was under the direction of Reverend Moody Hall until 1826, when on account of ill health, he retired from missionary work, and Reverend Daniel S. Buttrick assumed charge, continuing until 1836.

---

[*] Mss., Chamberlin.

[†] Missionary Herald, January, 1824, page 2.

[§] Taloney is the Cherokee word for dried sumac leaves, which was often mixed with tobacco for smoking purposes.

[‡] Missionary Herald, December, 1833.

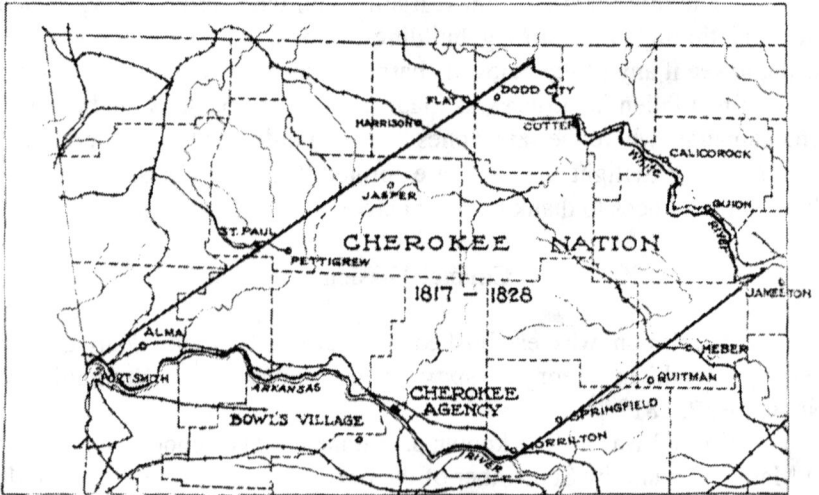

Map of the Cherokee Nation in Arkansas from 1817 to 1828.

Creek Path.

Miss Catherine Brown, a three-quarter blood Cherokee, aged 19 years, established Creek Path, near her home, in April, 1820. It was in Alabama, one hundred miles southwest of Brainard.

Reverend William Potter was assigned to Creek Path January 19, 1822, and stayed there until July, 1837.

Dr. Elizur Butler was attached to Creek Path on May 7, 1824, and remained until 1826.

Miss Ermine Nash of Cummington, Massachusetts, arrived at Creek Path November 5, 1825, staying there until 1837.

There were thirty-one pupils at Creek Path in 1828.

Creek Path belonged to the North Alabama Presbytery; in 1833 it had thirty-nine members.

Will's Town.

Willstown Mission, located in Will's Valley, Alabama, was founded March 28, 1823, by Reverend William Chamberlin, who had charge of this mission until 1839. He moved to Illinois, and died at Alton on March 14, 1849.[*]

Willstown was so named because it was the home of Will, an auburn haired, halfbreed Cherokee sub-chief.

Willstown was fifty miles southwest of Brainard, in Alabama, and was attached to the North Alabama Presbytery.

Reverend and Mrs. Ard Hoyt, the parents of Mrs. Chamberlin, arrived at Willstown, on May 22, 1824, and remained there until his death, which occurred on February 18., 1828. Mrs. Hoyt returned north in April, 1834.[†]

Hawais Mission.

Hawais Mission, originally called Turnip Mountain, in Georgia, was established in 1823 by Mr. John C. Ellsworth. It was attached to the Georgia Presbytery and in 1833 the church membership was fifty-eight.

Dr. Elizur Butler arrived at Hawais on May 1, 1826. Mrs. Dr. Butler, nee Esther Post, of South Concord, Connecticut, died at Hawais

---

[*] History of the Presbyterian Church in the State of Illinois, pages 300 to 307.

[†] Mss., Chamberlin.

on November 21, 1829. Dr. Butler married on August 14, 1830, Miss Lucy Ames, of Brainard Mission. She was a native of Groton, Massachusetts. He was arrested by the Georgia militia on July 7, 1831, for residing in the Cherokee Nation without a permit from Georgia; sentenced to penitentiary on September 16th of that year, and was released by the governor of Georgia, January 14th, 1833.

Hightower Mission.[‡]

Etowa Mission, improperly pronounced "Hightower," was founded in 1823, by Mr. and Mrs. Isaac Proctor, of New Hampshire. It was located on Etowa River, in Georgia, eighty miles southeast of Brainard and thirty-five miles west of Carmel. "Hightower" was attached to the Georgia Presbytery and in 1833 the church had twenty members.

Reverend Daniel S. Buttrick was attached to "Hightower" from 1827 to 1830.

Candy's Creek Mission.

Candy's Creek was founded in 1824 by William Holland and John Vail.

In 1828 there were thirty Cherokee pupils at this mission.

New Echota.[§]

This was the capitol of the Cherokee Nation. It was established as the capitol about 1818. The National Council authorized the erection of a building to be used as the office for the national newspaper, "The Cherokee Phoenix," on November 15, 1826.[*]

Reverend Samuel A. Worcester arrived at New Echota on November 27, 1827, and immediately commenced the work of translating the Scriptures into the Cherokee language. He immediately set to work to systematize the Sequoian syllabary, and shortly afterward perfected the phonetic arrangement as it is now known.

[‡] Missionary Herald, December, 1833; Missionary Herald, January, 1824, and Mss., Chamberlin.

[§] Now Rome, Georgia.

[*] Cherokee Laws, compilation of 1852, page 82.

New Echota was never used by the American Board as a mission, but a church was maintained and a great deal of religious literature was printed on the Phoenix press.

The first issue of the "Cherokee Phoenix," which was a weekly, was published on Thursday, February 21, 1828. The last issue was volume V, number 52, published May 31, 1834.

Elias Boudinot was the first editor of the "Phoenix." He resigned on August 1, 1832, and Chief Ross immediately appointed his own brother-in-law, Elijah Hicks.[*]

Reverend Samuel A. Worcester was arrested by the Georgia militia on July 7, 1831, on the charge of being in the Cherokee Nation without a permit from Georgia, and in violation of an act of the Georgia Legislature bearing date of December 22, 1830.[†] He was sentenced to the penitentiary on September 16, 1831, and was released by the governor on January 14, 1833. He returned to Brainard on March 15, 1834.

Dwight Mission.

In July, 1820, Reverends Cephas Washburn and Alfred Finney, accompanied by James Orr and Jacob Hitchcock, arrived in the "Western" Cherokee Nation, Arkansas Territory. Shortly afterwards they established Dwight Mission, on the west bank of Illinois Creek, four miles from Arkansas River. It was named in honor of Reverend Timothy Dwight, president of Yale College and the first signatory member of the American Board.

By the 1st of October, 1820, they had erected two "comfortable cabins," and soon afterwards Washburn and Finney returned to Elliott Mission, in Mississippi, for their families. They returned to Dwight on May 10, 1821.

They immediately commenced the erection of the school building, but before they finished it they ran out of nails and had to go to Union Mission (now in Mayes County, Oklahoma, over two hundred miles distance) to borrow enough to complete the building. The building was completed and school commenced on January 1, 1822.

---

[*] Senate document No. 121, Twenty-fifth Congress, second session; page 3.
[†] Laws of the Colonial and State governments relating to Indians, Washington, 1832.

Richard Taylor, Cherokee genealogy No. III—$1^1 2^2 3^3 1^4$.
Assistant Chief of the Cherokee Nation from November,
1851, to November, 1855.

EARLY HISTORY OF CHEROKEES.

In January, 1826, the following missionaries were at Dwight: Reverends Cephas Washburn and Alfred Finney, missionaries; Dr. George L. Weed, who afterwards moved to Cincinnati, Ohio, physician and teacher; Jacob Hitchcock, steward; Miss Cynthia Thrall, charge of school; Miss Ellen Stetson, teacher; James Orr, farmer; Samuel Wisner and Asa Hitchcock, mechanics.

Reverend and Mrs. Worcester Willey arrived at Dwight on January 31, 1826.

The "Western Cherokees" exchanged their land in Arkansas for land west of that territory, on May 6, 1828, and by the succeeding spring practically the entire Nation had moved to their new possession.

For that reason it became incumbent on the missionaries to also remove to the western territory. The entire missionary establishment of Dwight Mission was moved to and located on the site of Nicksville, the late county seat of Lovely County, Arkansas, in 1828 (on the west side of Sallisaw Creek, section 34, township 13, range 23, in the present county of Sequoyah, Oklahoma.

Reverend Daniel Sabin Buttrick arrived at Dwight in March, 1839.

Reverend William Potter, Dr. Elizur Butler and Miss Ermina Nash arrived at Dwight on June 10, 1839. Miss Nash was married at this mission on April 3, 1841, to Reverend Samuel A. Worcester.

Mrs. Alfred Finney, nee Susannah Washburn, a native of Randolph, Vermont, died at Dwight in January, 1833.

Dwight Mission has survived, with varying fortunes, to the present time.

Mulberry Mission.

Mulberry Mission was established on Mulberry Creek, in Pope County, Arkansas, in 1828, and was moved to a location some fifteen miles north of Dwight; its name was changed to Fairfield, and was under the direction of Reverend Dr. Marcus Palmer, who was transferred to this place from Union.

Union Mission.

This mission was established in 1820 by Reverend William F. Vail, of the United Foreign Missionary Society, for work among the Osages. It was located in what is now section 16, township 19 north, range 19 east, in Mayes County, Oklahoma. A large farm established in

1822 and run in connection with this school was called Hopefield. It was four miles from the main mission establishment and was under the direction of Reverend William B. Montgomery as missionary and George Requa as "superintendent of secular concerns."

The first Protestant conference, in what is now the state of Oklahoma, was held at Union Mission, from November 2nd to the 7th, 1822, the sessions being from 5:15 a. m. to 9 p. m. of each day, except the last, which ended shortly before noon. There were representatives from Union, Dwight and Harmony, which was located on the Maries des Cygnes River in Missouri. Reverend Benton Pixley of Harmony was chosen moderator, and Epaphrus Chapman, scribe.

As early as 1823 there were fourteen missionaries at this place, and the property was valued at $24,000.00.[*]

Dr. Marcus Palmer was granted a restricted license to preach on November 7, 1825, by a conference that was held at Union.

In January, 1826, the missionaries attached to Union were: Reverend William F. Vail, missionary; Dr. Marcus Palmer, physician; Stephen Fuller, Abraham Redfield, John M. Spaulding, Alexander Woodruff and George Requa, assistant missionaries, farmers and mechanics, and seven females. At this time they had twenty-six pupils.

In the fall of 1835, Reverend Samuel A. Worcester, arrived at Union and set up his mission press, on which was printed in December, 1835, the Cherokee Almanac for the year of 1836. As he moved to Park Hill on December 2, 1836, it is possible that no almanac was published for the year of 1837, but it was published at the latter place for each consecutive year thereafter, until 1861.

On May 10, 1826, the United Foreign Missionary Society and the American Board of Commissioners for Foreign Missions were united, and continued under the name of the latter organization.

Park Hill Mission.

Park Hill Mission was founded about 1829 by Samuel Newton, late of Osage Mission, in Kansas. He named the mission "Park Hill" on account of the natural beauty of its surroundings. His residence and mission was at "Campbell's Spring,"[†] between the later residences of

---

[*] Missionary Herald.

[†] SE¼ NE¼ NE¼ Section 22, Township 16 North, Range 22 East in Cherokee County.

Chief John Ross and Reverend Samuel A. Worcester. The mission was later moved to a location about a quarter of a mile east of the residence of Reverend Worcester, and at this latter place the mission press was established.

Mr. Newton afterwards moved to Washington County, Arkansas, and was postmaster of Boonsborough in 1847.

Rev. Samuel A. Worcester and his first wife, nee Ann Orr, a native of Bedford, New Hampshire, both died and were buried at Park Hill.

The Parkhill Mission was in operation at the time of the coming of the Emigrant Cherokees, in 1839, and for many years afterwards.

The Mission at the forks of the Illinois.

This mission was in operation in 1830 and is perpetuated in the present Elm Springs Mission.

Methodist Missions.

The policy of the Methodists was not to build large mission establishments as the Presbyterians did. Their work was more along evangelical lines, primary instruction being subsidiary.

In 1822, at the solicitation of Richard Riley, a half blood Cherokee, Reverend Richard Neely, of the Tennessee Methodist Conference, commenced to preach in the Cherokee country. Riley and several others joined the church during this year.[*]

Reverends I. W. Sullivan and Ambrose F. Driskill succeeded Neely. John Fletcher Boot, a full blood Cherokee, was licensed to preach by the Tennessee Conference and the first mission school was established in 1824.[†]

In 1825 Reverends F. A. Owen, Ambrose F. Driskill and Richard Neely each had supervision of a mission school, but neither their names nor locations are given.[‡]

In 1826 a fourth mission was added. It was placed under the supervision of Reverend William McMahon. During this year, Turtle Fields, an eighth blood Cherokee veteran of the Creek war of 1812-14,

---

[*] Handbook of Methodist Missions. I. G. Johns, Nashville, Tenn., 1893, pages 109-110.

[†] Handbook of Methodist Missions, page 110.

[‡] Handbook of Methodist Missions, page 110.

was converted.

In 1827 Reverend William McMahon was superintendent of Cherokee missions, of which there were seven, one being under the charge of Reverend Turtle Fields. The church had six hundred and seventy-five members at the close of this year.[§]

In the fall of 1828 the Tennessee Conference made the following appointments for the Cherokee Nation:

Superintendent of Missions, Reverend William McMahon.

Wills Valley and Oostanalla, Reverend John B. McFerrin, with Joseph Blackbird as interpreter.

Coosawatee,[‡] Reverend Turtle Fields.

Mount Wesley and Asbury, Reverend Dixon C. McLeod. A school attached.

Chatooga, Reverend Greenbury Garrett. A school attached.

Sulacooie, Reverend Nicholas Dalton Scales. A school attached.

Neely's Grove, Reverend Allen F. Scruggs. A school attached.

Conasauga, Reverend Thomas J. Elliott. A school attached.

General missionary to travel through the Nation, Reverend James Jenkins Trott.

Chief John Ross joined the Methodist Church, and Reverend Richard Neely died during this year. The Church membership reached to seven hundred and thirty-six, and one year later it was one thousand and twenty-eight.[*]

I have purposely gone into details in giving the narratives of the several missionary efforts, having two points in view. The first was to show that the missionary propaganda among the Cherokees had been of respectable proportions, and for that reason and through the respect that was engendered by the missionaries, the Cherokees embraced the civilizing and refining influence of the churches and missions and by 1830 were practically a civilized race, the transposition taking place in the first thirty years of the Nineteenth Century. The second was the laying of the foundations for the history of the future educational progress of the Cherokees.

[§] Handbook of Methodist Missions, page 111.

[‡] Cherokee for Old Creek Town.

[*] John B. McFerrin, a Biography, by Rev. O. P. Fitzgerald, 1889, pages 114-115.

GOVERNMENTAL AID TO THE MISSIONS.

By an act of Congress in the year of 1819 an appropriation was made to aid the civilization of Indian tribes. Among the other tribes that were beneficiaries of the distribution, the Cherokees were fortunate in being included. This money was paid directly to the several missionary schools for buildings, improvements and annuities in quarterly installments. For some ten or twelve years these approximate annuities among others were paid to the missionaries having charge of these several missions:

Brainard Mission, allowed..........................$1,000.00
Dwight   "   " 800.00
Valley Town "   " 500.00
Spring Place "   " 300.00
Tinsawatee   "   " 250.00

CHARACTER OF THE CHEROKEES.

"The Cherokees intermarried more freely with the whites than did the other tribes, and with exceptional results. The half-breed Cherokees were a fine race physically, exhibiting the best characteristics of both races. The men were tall and well formed, and the women, with their queenly carriage, brilliant dark eyes, clear complexion, expressive features and vivacity tempered by a natural dignity peculiar to themselves, were remarkable for their beauty. The weak and strong points of both races are visible in their moral constitution. They are by turns generous, moody, brave, suspicious, true to friends, and implacable to foes, with a tragic element that flames out with terrific energy when least expected."[†] The description of the Cherokees was given by a man who had been a Methodist circuit rider in the Cherokee Nation in 1828 and 1829. He lived in the Cherokee Nation during this time and boarded with a Cherokee family. Reverend A. N. Chamberlin, the son of Reverend William Chamberlin, had been reared in the Cherokee country, had a comprehensive knowledge of their language and history, and for that reason his statement in regard to the Cherokees is invaluable. He said, "It is worthy of remark that in no ignorant country have the missionaries experienced less trouble and difficulty in spreading a

[†] John B. McFerrin, a Biography, page 63.

knowledge of the Bible than in this. Here, they have been welcomed and encouraged by the proper authorities of the Nation; their persons have been protected, and in very few instances have some individual vagabonds threatened violence to them.

"The Cherokees have had no established religion of their own, and perhaps to this circumstance we may attribute, in part, the facilities with which missionaries have pursued their ends."[‡]

GENESIS OF CIVILIZATION.

Several of the mixed blooded Cherokees were cultured, refined and educated; but the great mass of people were still in their aboriginal state, as was evidenced by the following description of a delegation that was preparing to visit Washington on official business in 1817. "Their ears were slitted, after the Indian manner, and pieces of silver were attached to them. Their dress was the hunting shirt, vest, turban, deerskin leggings, with silk or other garters and moccasins. Some of them had hats. One of them showed me a pair of silver spurs, made by a native, which were very elegant. The price of them was eleven dollars. They were true specimens of native ingenuity. The chiefs were all well provided with horses, saddles and blankets. Their appearance was that of utmost contentment."[*]

The fourteenth article of the United States-Cherokee treaty of July 2, 1791, concluded on Holston River in Tennessee, specified "That the Cherokee Nation may be led to a greater degree of civilization, and to become herdsmen and cultivators, instead of remaining in a state of hunters. The United States will, from time to time, furnish, gratuitously, the said Nation with useful implements of husbandry."

By a census taken in 1819 it was shown that the Cherokees had "19,500 cattle, 6,100 horses, 19,600 swine, 1,037 sheep, 467 looms, 1,600 spinning wheels, 39 wagons, 500 ploughs, 13 grist mills and 3 saw mills."[†]

The progress of the Cherokees was such that on May 30, 1820, Return J. Meigs, the United States agent for the Cherokees since 1801,

---

[‡] Mss., Chamberlin.
[*] Memoirs of Elias Cornelius, page 76.
[†] Mss., Chamberlin.

wrote the Secretary of War: "That Government aid is no longer necessary or desirable; that the Cherokees are perfectly competent to take care of themselves, and that further contributions to their support only has a tendency to encourage idleness and dependence upon the government."

On April 30, 1838, Senator Wilson Lumpkin of Georgia, who had been governor of his state during a portion of the time that it was embroiled with the Cherokee troubles, addressed the Senate, and in the course of his address said: "During the Revolutionary War, and at its close, there were Tories who fled from the just indignation of their countrymen to escape the punishment due to their crimes, and joined the Cherokee Indians, and fought by their sides, amalgamated with them, took their daughters for wives, and took up their permanent residence among them. One of these was a Scotchman by the name of Daniel Ross, and the father of the celebrated John Ross. Some of these men had property, education and intelligence, and soon acquired great influence amongst the Indians, and in many cases were careful to educate their children from their Indian wives. These men and their descendants taught the Southern Indians many of the arts of husbandry and industry, and imparted to them their first ideas of a system of government and laws which would secure individual rights and property. Thus they acquired a knowledge of the first principles of human prosperity. Civil order and law being thus introduced, they, by slow degrees, continued to improve. The circumstances, too, of their having for a long time a very large territory, unintruded upon by the Whites, was favorable to their imbibing lofty feelings of a character and independence which is indispensable to the political advancement of any people. These improvements thus made in the condition of the Southern Indians greatly facilitated the operations of the missionaries who settled in their country at a subsequent period. These missionaries were not placed among a people altogether savage, but always took up their abodes in the neighborhoods far advanced in civilization.

"Many of the Indians and 'Indian countrymen' had good houses and farms and large herds of cattle, sheep and hogs, household furniture, implements of husbandry, besides a number of Negro slaves. The missionaries, in settling among such a people as I have described, found a state of society not widely differing from that which, in former days, might often be found in countries now settled by civilized men. Some of the missionaries who settled among the Cherokees were good people, and were very useful to the natives; but at the same time, most of them advanced their own circumstances and comfort, and improved their own conditions from what they had been accustomed to full as much as they improved the churches.

"These missionary efforts in the Cherokee country have been greatly exaggerated, and gone forth to the world in religious magazines and various other forms, and will most likely be handed down to posterity, and pervert the truth on the historic page when the present generation shall have passed away. Be assured, sirs, that the greatly improved condition of the Cherokee people cannot be primarily attributed to missionary labor, but to the establishment of law and civil order, produced by means to which I have already adverted."[*]

JOHN ROSS.

John Ross was one-eighth Cherokee and seven-eighths Scotch. His father was Daniel Ross, his grandfather was John McDonald and his great grandfather was William Shorey, all Scotchmen. On the maternal line John Ross belonged to the Bird clan. He was born at Turkeytown, on Coosa River, on October 3, 1790. He was educated privately by George Barbee Davis of Marysville, Tennessee, and later at Kingston, Tennessee.

He was deputized by the United States agent to the Cherokees, Return Jonathan Meigs, to visit the Western Cherokees, who then lived between the Arkansas and White rivers in Arkansas, with presents, in order to be certain of their neutrality in the struggle with Great Britain. This trip embraced four months, from December 25, 1812, to April, 1813. Shortly after his return from this trip he married Quatie, a full Cherokee, of his own, the Bird clan.[*] She was born in 1791.

He was adjutant in Morgan's Cherokee regiment of United States allies in the "Creek War" of 1813-14.

He was president of the National Committee from October 5, 1818, to November 15, 1826. He was Second Chief of the Cherokees

---

[*] Removal of the Cherokee Indians from Georgia, 1827-1838; Wilson Lumpkin, Volume 11, pages 195-196.

[*] Had such a marriage occurred twenty years earlier they would have been executed.

(East) from 1826 to 1828. He was a member of the Cherokee Constitutional Convention from Chicamauga District, president of the convention and drafted the Constitution of July 26, 1827. He was elected principal chief of the Cherokee Nation (East) on October 13, 1828, and was re-elected by the vote of "less than two hundred" members of the convention and council in August, 1832.[†] This was his last election by the Cherokee Nation east of the Mississippi River.

He was "fully authorized and empowered to make such requisitions for money as from time to time he may deem necessary for the Cherokee emigration, upon such officers of the United States Government as may have control of the funds for this service, and to receipt for the same for the Cherokee Nation." The date of appointment was August 1, 1838.[‡] His wife, Quatie, died enroute west, on February 1, 1839, and was buried in Little Rock, Arkansas.

He signed the "Act of Union" of the Eastern and Western Cherokees on July 12, 1839, as "Principal Chief of the Eastern Cherokees."

He was elected Principal Chief of the Cherokee Nation by the Constitutional Convention on September 9, 1839. He was regularly re-elected in 1843, 1847, 1851, 1855 and 1859.

He married on September 2, 1844, Mary Brian Stapler, born in New Castle County, Delaware. She died in July, 1865. He died at Washington, D. C., on August 1, 1866.

Physically Mr. Ross was about five feet seven inches in height, straight, symmetrical, had black hair, grey eyes, florid complexion, and was always faultlessly dressed. While he most probably understood the Cherokee language, he always made use of the most choice English in expressing his thoughts and used a Cherokee interpreter when necessary.

On May 1, 1852, Governor Lumpkin wrote the following estimate of Chief Ross: "From my first acquaintance with John Ross, now upwards of thirty years ago, I was sensible of his superior cultivation and intellectual advantages. He is a well educated man—converses well, writes well, and is a man of soft, easy, gentlemanly manners, rather retiring and reserved; seldom speaks unadvisedly. In all the common duties and intercourse of life he has always maintained a

---

[†] Senate Document No. 121, 25th Congress, 2nd Session, page 34.
[‡] House of Representatives Document No. 129, 26th Congress, 1st Session, page 36.

John Ross and Signature. Cherokee genealogy No. XVI—
$1^1 1^2 1^3 3^4$. Principal Chief of the Cherokee Nation from
1827 to 1866.

good moral character. His position in life, from first to last, has afforded him every facility to gain information and add to his stock of knowledge. "Although he did not come to the **throne** by regular hereditary descent, yet very many circumstances pointed to him, from early boyhood, as the prospective ruler of the Cherokees; and he has governed them in the most absolute manner for upwards of a quarter of a century, by seeming to obey. A full examination of the records of the Federal Government will show that John Ross has had the entire control and disbursement of millions of dollars, as king of the Cherokees, during the last twenty years. The control of this immense amount of money, in the absence of any enlightened supervision or check on his financial aspirations, is the key that unlocks the secret cause of his long career of absolute reign and power, as well as his great popularity at home and abroad."[*]

In a letter to General Winfield Scott, dated April 7, 1838, Senator Lumpkin said of John Ross: "Ross is the soul and spirit of his whole party, and they will act in accordance with his views. In regard to Ross himself, he is a sagacious, subtle man. Under the guise of an unassuming deportment, his arrogance is unsurpassed. He always takes high ground, and maintains the most dignified reserve, and never communicates freely and without reserve even with his best friends. He has the art of acquiring credit for talents and wisdom which he never possessed.

"He writes well, but has had the credit of being the author of many able productions which were written by others, and not himself. Some of the first writers of the age, such a[sic] Sergeant of Philadelphia, Wirt of Virginia, etc., etc., have long been his feed counsel, and have suffered their pens to be brought into requisition in aid of this man Ross."[†]

Mr. Ross had an odd habit in writing his state and semi-state papers and letters that I don't believe had a duplicate in the writings of any other public man.

It was his custom to write most of the state papers of the Cherokee Nation himself, seldom delegating this work to a clerk or amanuensis. They were written in very legible long hand. He wrote his

---

[*] Removal of the Cherokee Indians from Georgia, Volume 1, pages 186-187.
[†] Removal of the Cherokee Indians from Georgia, Volume 11, pages 229-230.

first copy, which was always couched in splendid English, and would have satisfied most men; but he then went over this copy, cutting out redundancies, interlining corrections and new thoughts, refining the general sense, and finally making the second copy, embodying the corrections. Then for a second time it would be gone over carefully as before, and occasionally the fourth copy would be made before he was satisfied. Then a copy of this last letter would be made and forwarded to its destination. He would then roll the other copies together and file them, as, I suppose, for originals. Many of these odd little rolls can be found in big boxes at the residence of his grandson, Hon. Robert B. Ross, at Tahlequah.

GEORGIA CONTROVERSY.

By the terms of an agreement that was made by "commissioners appointed on the part of the United States" and "commissioners appointed on the part of the State of Georgia," under date of April 24, 1804, the United States Government in consideration of a cession of a large portion of the western territory of Georgia, agreed to extinguish the Indians' title and claim to all of the lands that were included within certain metes and bounds that was considered by all the delegates as being justly portions of Georgia.

Much of the land referred to was at that time, and remained until 1838, in the possession of Cherokee Indians.

Georgia was naturally insistent that the stipulations of this agreement be carried into effect at the earliest possible moment.

The Cherokees, who held this land by fifteen treaties[*] with the United States, had not been parties to, nor did they have knowledge of the United States-Georgia agreement for some time after it was consummated.

The Cherokees were reluctant to cede their reservation and a grim travesty was that as they became more enlightened and prosperous they furnished a greater reason why Georgia should become more anxious to be rid of them as a foreign and unaffiliated nation. If they had remained an uncivilized nation, it would have been much easier to

---

[*] Treaties of Sept. 28, 1785; July 2, 1791; June 26, 1794; October 2, 1798; October 24, 1804; October 25, 1805; October 27, 1805; January 7, 1806; September 11, 1807; February 22, 1816; February 22, 1817; September 14, 1816; July 8, 1817; February 27, 1819, and May 6, 1828.

negotiate and deal with them; but when they began to know their rights they commenced to defend them before Congress, the bench and the bar of public opinion.

The first law that we have any record of as having been enacted by the Cherokees then living east of the Mississippi River was that of September 11, 1808, at Broom's Town.[||]

The second recorded Cherokee law bore the date of April 10, 1810, and was enacted at a council sitting at Oostanallah.[†] Black Fox was Principal Chief in both instances.

The third known act was of more consequence, as it was distinctly constitutional in character.[‡]

New Town or New Echota, became the capitol of the Cherokee Nation at some time between May 6, 1817, and October 26, 1819,[§] as the latter was the first date on which it was mentioned as the capitol.

On October 20, 1820, the council of the Cherokee Nation made provision for the erection of eight civil and judicial districts in the Cherokee Nation,[**] and either at the beginning of or at some time prior to the convening of the next regular council the boundaries of the proposed districts were submitted and accepted.[††]

The many laws and resolutions necessary to the founding of a civil government for the Cherokees were drafted and enacted at the regular sessions of their national councils, which met on the first Monday of October of each year and remained in session for four weeks or more.

The Council enacted a resolution on October 13, 1826, providing for the election in each of the eight districts of delegates that were to assemble at New Echota on the 4th day of July, 1827, and form a Constitution for the Cherokee Nation.[‡‡]

In accordance with the provisions of the resolution, the duly elected constitutional delegates met, and after mature deliberation they adopted a constitution,[§§] the main draft of which is generally accredited

---

[||] Page 180.
[†] Page 181.
[‡] Page 182.
[§] Laws of the Cherokee Nation compilation of 1852, page 4.
[**] Page 185.
[††] Page 186.
[‡‡] Page 196.
[§§] Page 200.

Mrs. Samuel M. Wear, nee Miss Susie McClellan. Cherokee genealogy No. IV—$1^1 9^2 7^3 4^4$.

with having been the work of John Ross. This was the first aboriginal American constitution.

Thus it will be seen that at the beginning of 1828 the Cherokees had a republican form of government based on a constitution, a national newspaper* which defended its rights, several opulent, intelligent and energetic citizens, and the nation was represented at Washington during each Congress by Chief John Ross.

Georgia memoralized[sic] Congress, asking that the United States make all possible haste in extinguishing the Cherokee claims to portions of Georgia as had been promised. The United States found that their pleas for cessions of Cherokee lands in Georgia were futile.

Georgia protested, Georgia threatened war, Georgia was ably championed by the popular and forcible Jackson.

The Cherokee question became a political issue and the great Whig orators bitterly assailed Jackson and his stand for the "dispossessing of the poor Cherokees."

Chief Ross, writers employed or interested by him, the missionaries and Whig partisans exerted every effort to spread the anti-Georgia propaganda by the forum and through the papers of the East. Voluminous protests poured in on Congress from individuals and legislatures.

Behind all suavely, apparently reserved and unobtrusive, stood John Ross, Chief of the Cherokees and consummate diplomat.

The fog that he cast over what might have been critical public opinion was so pervading that even to this day the close and careful historical student begins to halt and grope when he enters this perplexing period.

A census of the Cherokees that remained east of the Mississippi River in 1835 showed that there were 16,542 Cherokees. 201 intermarried Whites, and that they owned 1,592 Negroes. At that time over one-third of the Cherokees were west of the Mississippi, among whom were some of the largest slaveholders.

A letter from Benjamin Gold, the father of Mrs. Elias Boudinot, to his brother, Hezekiah, gives some interesting views of conditions in the Cherokee Nation in 1829.

Gold and his wife had made the trip from Cornwall, Connecticut,

---

* The Cherokee Phoenix.

to New Echota in a one-horse wagon. After having corrected many of his errors in spelling, I give you the letter, with corrective notes in italics:

NEW ECHOTA IN 1829.

Dear Brother:

We arrived here on the 27th day of October, *1829*. Forty-seven days on our journey. We might have performed the journey sooner, but we chose not to be in haste and to give ourselves time to view the country, and get acquainted with the people on the way, and moderately drive our horse, as a thousand miles is a pretty serious journey for a horse, and to carry as much of a load as we had. But by a merciful Providence we were upheld and wonderfully supported all the way, in good health and good spirits. We are now in good health and can say with truth that now, nearly three months since we left home, has been as pleasant and interesting as any part of our lives.

We traveled through a very pleasant part of the country, from Newburgh through Orange County into New Jersey; then into Pennsylvania, then through a small part of Maryland, and over the Potomac about thirty miles north of Baltimore, then into the great state of Virginia four hundred miles; then into Tennessee two hundred miles, then crossed Hiwassee River at a place called Calhoun, into the Cherokee Nation, where an agent of the United States resides to manage the affairs of the Cherokee Nation.

We put up at the house of Mr. Lewis Ross, one of the principal chiefs of the Cherokee Nation. It being a rainy day we tarried there two nights. *Lewis Ross was a prominent citizen, but was never a chief.* His home is an elegant white house near the bank of the river, as neatly furnished as almost any house in Litchfield County. His family of four pretty children, the eldest a daughter of about eighteen years, attending a high school in Tennessee, appears as well as any girl of her age. Mr. Ross, *who is* a brother of the Chief, *John Ross,* has two or three large stores, no doubt independent, has Negroes enough to wait on us. He made us feel very welcome, and said he would take nothing from anyone who had connections in the Nation.

He is part Cherokee, *one-eighth blood*; his wife is a white woman of the Meigs family, but you would not suspect him or his children to be of Indian blood.

We then traveled about twenty miles and came to a Mr. McNair's, a white man who had married a Cherokee Indian woman, sister of Mr. Joseph Vann, another Cherokee chief. *Mr. Vann was not a chief, this was a common error with people that did not know.* He had a beautiful white house, and about six or seven hundred acres of the best land you ever saw, and Negroes enough to tend it and clear as much more as he pleased. He raised this year about five thousand bushels of corn, and it would make you feel small to see his situation. Mr. Vann lives in a large brick house elegantly furnished. We staid[sic] there over night, and he would take nothing of us. We have considerable acquaintance with some of the principal men of the Nation. We were here two or three weeks while the council was in session, and were introduced to all of them and became familiar with most of them. We have traveled about one hundred miles in the Nation, visited three mission stations and are much pleased with the missionaries. We have met and become acquainted with most of them.

Mr. Boudinot has much good company, and is as much respected as any man of his age. His paper, *The Phoenix,* is known and respected all over the United States and in Europe. He has about one hundred newspapers sent him from different parts of the United States by way of exchange, so that you perceive we have an interesting stand where we have the news from all quarters of the globe. We are in good health, likewise Mr. Boudinot and family.

They have two beautiful and interesting children: Eleanor Susan, born May 24, 1827, and Mary Harriette, born October 5, 1828. They would pass in company for full blooded Yankees. My wife says that she thinks they are rather handsomer than any she has seen in the North. Am uncertain when we shall return to Connecticut.

Harriette *(Mrs. Boudinot)* says she well remembers the conversation with Dr. Gold, when he labored with her to dissuade her from her purpose; he supposing that she was going to place herself in an unhappy situation. But she wishes you to present her regards to the Doctor, and tell him that she has never yet seen the time that she regretted coming here in the manner she did, but has ever rejoiced that she placed herself here; that she envies the situation of no one in Connecticut.

She has a large and convenient frame house, two stories, forty by fifty on the ground, well finished and furnished with the comforts of life.

They get their supplies of clothes and groceries from Boston and Augusta, Georgia. They have their year's supply of both. They keep a supply of two or three barrels of flour on hands[sic] at once.

This neighborhood is truly an interesting and pleasant place. The ground is as level and smooth as a floor; the center of the Nation; a new place laid out in city form; a hundred lots of an acre each.* A spring, called the public spring, about twice as large as our saw mill brook, near the center, with other springs on the plot; six new frame houses in sight, besides a council house, court house, *Phoenix* printing office and four stores, all in sight of Mr. Boudinot's house. The stores are continued only during the session of the Council and then removed to other parts of the Nation, except one, which is steadily continued. The stores of the Nation are as large as the best in our towns in Litchfield County. Their large wagons of six horses go to Augusta and bring a great load; and you will see a number of them together. There is much travel through this place.

I have seen eleven of these large wagons pass by Mr. Boudinot's in company.

John Ridge was clerk of the Cherokee council, and is now clerk of a Creek delegation to Congress for the winter, and will likely get his five or ten thousand as he did before. The Cherokee delegation has gone to Congress again this winter. I could tell you many pleasant things about the country, but for fear that you may not be able to read, or get tired, I must close by telling you that you must give our love to your family and friends, and accept the kind regards of your affectionate brother,

BENJAMIN GOLD.

The above given letter is not an exact literal copy, but adheres to the sense of the original, which is to a degree idiomatic.

Through the indefatigable work of Reverend Samuel A. Worcester and Mr. Elias Boudinot, there was printed in Cherokee, on the Phoenix press, by 1833, fourteen thousand six hundred and fifty religious books.*

---

* Established by Act of National Council, November 12, 1825. See Cherokee Laws, compilation of 1852, pages 62 and 63.
* Mss., Chamberlin.

EMIGRATION SENTIMENT.

On account of the steady encroachments of the white settlers and of the policies of the neighboring states, the retention of their homes, by the "Eastern" Cherokees, had to the unprejudiced and more reasonable portion of the tribe, become apparent, as only a short respite.[†]

The great majority of the "Eastern" Cherokees were at that time full bloods, and they followed the fortunes of their great arbiter, John Ross, who always directed the policies of the Nation as his followers wished them to be. Whenever a member of the council resigned or was expelled, Chief Ross appointed one of his partisans in his stead, and in this way their boasted representative government soon became an empty farce.

So many of the Cherokees had seen the lowering clouds of destruction hanging over their Nation that they had emigrated to the Cherokee Nation in Arkansas Territory and beyond; so many, in fact, that by 1835 it was computed that one-third of the tribe was living March 4, 1905 in the nation west of the Mississippi River. Even William Shorey Coody, the brilliant and talented nephew and right hand man of Chief John Ross, had settled in the "West"; this man who was commonly supposed to be the heir apparent, as much as a man might be heir apparent, in a republic, to the chieftaincy.[†]

Despairing of any action by the regularly constituted chief, in making any provision for meeting the certain violent dissolution of their country, a small minority of the more intelligent "Eastern" Cherokees, that were not under the dominion and sway of Chief Ross, met a representative of the United States at Red Clay, Georgia, and made a treaty with him on December 29, 1835, by which they ceded to the United States all of the Cherokee lands east of Mississippi River for a consideration of five million dollars.

From this time until the Civil War, the political lines between the Ross or Anti-Treaty, and the Anti-Ross, or Ridge parties, were closely drawn; and after the treaty party had come west and joined the "Old Settler" Cherokees, as those who had emigrated to the west side of the

---

[†] Senate Document No. 121, 25th Congress, 2nd Session, page 2.

[†] William Shorey Coody, the author of the Cherokee Constitution of 1839, died April 16, 1849, aged 42 years.

Mississippi River before the consummation of the treaty of 1835 were called, a common interest brought them together in opposition to the Anti-Treaty or Ross party.

Although under the provisions of the Cherokee Constitution of 1827, a chief's election was to be held once every four years by the joint vote of the council; on account of the general unrest and uncertainty in the "Eastern" Cherokee Nation, no election was held after October, 1829.[‡]

WESTERN CHEROKEES.

In May, 1782, a delegation of Cherokees applied to Don Estevan Miro, Governor of Louisiana, for permission to settle on the west side of the Mississippi River in Spanish territory, and their request was granted. It is probable that some of them availed themselves of this permission, and it is quite likely that they were already residents of Upper Louisiana, and only made this request to confirm their rights.

In a report written at "St. Luis de Ylinnesses" (St. Louis of Illinois, the present St. Louis, Mo.) on December 10, 1775, by Francisco Cruzat[‖] to Don Luis de Unzaga y Amazaga, Governor of Louisiana, said: "Since the Cheraquis Indians compelled the miners at the Mine de Mota,[*] located fifteen leagues from St. Genoveva, to abandon it."[†]

Black Hawk, in his autobiography, states that he was a member of a band of Sac and Foxes who, in 1787, engaged a band of Cherokees on Merrimac River, in Missouri; in which his father, who was chief of the band, was killed, and the Cherokees were defeated with a loss of twenty-eight men.

In an encounter at Mussel Shoals, Tennessee, in June, 1794, between a number of Cherokees from Running Water Town, under the leadership of Bowl, and some boatmen, the Cherokees killed all of the

---

[‡] Constitution of the Cherokee Nation, 1827, Article IV, Section I: The Supreme Executive Power of this Nation shall be vested in a Principal Chief, who shall be chosen by the General Council, and shall hold his office four years; to be elected as follows: The General Council by a joint vote, shall, at their second annual session, after the rising of this Convention, and at every fourth annual session thereafter, on the second day after the Houses shall be organized, and competent to proceed to business, elect a Principal Chief.

[‖] Lieutenant-governor of Louisiana.

[*] Mine La Motte is at the head of St. Francis River in Madison County, Missouri.

[†] Spanish Regime in Missouri, Volume 11, Chicago, 1909; Louis Houck.

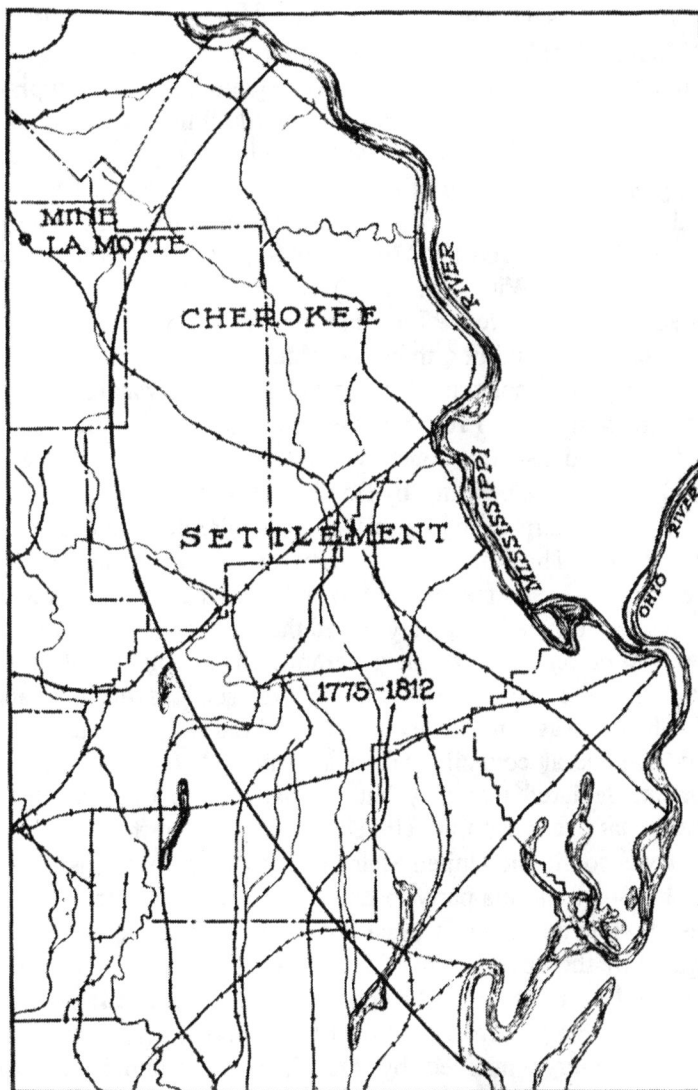

Map of the Cherokee Settlement in Missouri.

boatmen.[‡]

Washburn says that "After this bloody tragedy, which is known as the Mussel Shoals Massacre, the whole party of Cherokees went aboard the boats, descended the Tennessee, Ohio and Mississippi to the mouth of St. Francis River. There they placed all the white women and children in one boat, relinquished to them all the furniture which they claimed, granted to each one of the married ladies a female servant, put on board an ample stock of provisions and four strong and able black men and let them descend the Mississippi to New Orleans, the place of their destination. With one of these ladies I afterward became acquainted. At her residence I have frequently domiciled when visiting New Orleans, and found her, though a widow, truly 'a mother in Israel.' She was to New Orleans what Mrs. Isabella Graham was to New York. It was from her lips that I received the foregoing particulars. She often spoke of the kindness and courtesy with which she and all the white ladies and children were treated by Bowl and his party.

"But to return to my narrative. After the departure of the boat for New Orleans, The Bowl and his party ran the other boats, with their contents of goods, servants, etc., a few miles up the St. Francis River to await the issue of the affair. They feared that their conduct at the Mussel Shoals would be regarded by our government as a violation of the treaty of amity and as a renewal of hostility. As soon as the massacre of Mussel Shoals was known to the Cherokees in their towns, they convened a general council, and in a memorial to the United States government, declared that they had no part in the tragedy; that they wished to be at peace with the United States, and that they would do all in their power to aid the United States in bringing them to justice. They sent to The Bowl and his party to return and submit to a trial for taking the lives of white citizens of United States. When this whole matter was investigated by the government of the United States the Cherokees were fully justified and the property confiscated and declared by treaty to belong justly to the perpetrators of the Mussel Shoals Massacre.

"The course pursued by the Cherokee Council toward the refugees tended to alienate their minds from their people in the home of their fathers, and made them less reluctant to remain in their new homes

---

[‡] Haywood's Civil and Political History of Tennessee. Washburn's Reminiscences; Letter 1.

west of the Mississippi. Added to this, the abundance of game, the fertility of the soil, and the blandness of the climate, soon made them prefer their homes here to those where they had resided in the east. Other parties, who crossed the Mississippi for the purpose of hunting and trapping, when they saw the prosperity of these original refugees, joined them. In 1812, by an arrangement of the government, they removed from St. Francis and settled between Arkansas and White rivers. In 1813, a considerable accession was made to their number by voluntary emigration from the old Nation, and they became so numerous that an agent of the United States was sent to reside among them. Until the whole tribe were united west of the State of Arkansas in 1839, they were known and treated with as the 'Arkansas Cherokees' or the "Cherokee Nation West." By the treaty of Turkeytown, in 1817, the government stipulated to give the Arkansas Cherokees as much land, "acre for acre," between the Arkansas and White rivers, as they would cede of their domain in the east, besides paying the emigrants for their improvements, transport them to their new homes, subsist them for twelve months after their arrival, besides other perquisites and valuable considerations. The result of this treaty was a considerable emigration from the east to the west in the years 1818 and 1819. From that time till their union by the treaty of 1835, which was not effected, in fact, till 1839, the Arkansas Cherokees were estimated at one-third of the whole tribe. Thus I have given you a succinct account of the origin of the 'Cherokee Nation West.' I have omitted many details for the sake of brevity."[*]

These continued migrations did not meet with the approval of the authorities of the Cherokee Nation, "East," as may be evinced by the following laws"

"Resolved by the National Committee and Council, That any person or persons, whatsoever, who shall choose to emigrate to the Arkansas country, and shall sell the improvements he or they may be in possession of, to any person or persons whatsoever, he or they, so disposing of their improvemnts[sic] shall forfeit and pay unto the Cherokee Nation the sum of one hundred and fifty dollars; and be it further

"Resolved, That any person or persons whatsoever, who shall purchase any improvemnts[sic] from any person or persons so emigrating,

---

[*] Washburn's Reminiscences, Letter 1.

he or they, so offending, shall also forfeit and pay a fine of one hundred and fifty dollars to the Nation, to be collected by the marshal of the district. By order of the National Committee.

JOHN ROSS, President National Committee.

ALEXANDER McCOY, Clerk National Committee.

Approved: October 27th, 1821.

His

PATH x KILLER.

Mark

Chas. R. Hicks.[†]

Resolved by the National Committee and Council, in General Council Convened, That from and after the passage of this act, if any citizens of the Nation shall bind themselves by enrollment or otherwise as emigrants to Arkansa[sic], or for the purpose of removing out of the jurisdictional limits of the Nation, he, she or they so enrolling or otherwise binding themselves, shall forfeit thereby all the rights and privileges he, she or they may have previously thereto claimed or enjoyed as citizens of this Nation and shall be viewed in the same light as others not entitled to citizenship, and treated accordingly.

Be it further resolved, That if any person or persons, citizens of this Nation, shall sell or dispose of his, her or their improvements to any person or persons so enrolled or otherwise bound as above mentioned, he, she or they, shall be viewed as having disposed of his, her or their improvements to a citizen of the United States, and shall be ineligible to hold any office of honor, profit or trust in this Nation, and upon conviction thereof, before any of the circuit courts of the several districts, be fined in a sum not less than one thousand dollars, nor exceeding two thousand dollars, and be punished with one hundred lashes.

Be it further resolved, In order to prevent any person or persons from screening him, her or them from the penalties above prescribed by pretending to have sold or disposed of his, her or their improvements to a lawful citizen and not an emigrant, all citizens of this Nation who may hereafter buy, sell or dispose of in any manner their improvements to each other, be, and they are hereby required, the disposer as well as the purchaser of such improvements, to make affidavit, to be filed in the clerk's office of the district, before any of the District Judges or Clerks of

---

[†] Laws of the Cherokee Nation, Compilation of 1852, page 19.

the several courts, that he, she or they did not dispose of or transfer, purchase or obtain any improvement for the purpose of having it valued by the United States commissioners or agents, or were not acting as agents or emigrants in making such purchase or transfer, and in case any such person or persons shall fail to comply with this requirement, such person or persons shall, upon conviction before any of the Circuit Courts of the nation, pay a fine of not less than one dollar; nor exceeding two hundred dollars, for every offense so committed.

Be it further resolved, That if any citizen or citizens of this Nation shall dispose of or transfer his, her or their improvements without complying with the requirements of the third section of this act, and the person or persons to whom the sale or transfer of such improvements may be made, should thereafter by enrollment or otherwise become an emigrant or emigrants, and shall get said improvement or improvements valued by the agents of the General Government, within thirty days after such purchase or transfer shall have been made, or at any time whilst the disposer continues to remain in possession of the same, then, in that case, the person or persons who may have so disposed of or transferred the improvements as aforesaid, shall be subject to the same penalty prescribed in the second section of this act, for disposing of improvements to emigrants.

Be it further resolved, That any person or persons, whosoever, who have bound themselves together by enrollment or otherwise as emigrants under the treaty of 1828, with the Arkansas Cherokees, or who have had, or intend to have their improvements valued by the agents of the General Government, and do not remove out of the jurisdictional limits of this Nation within fifteen days after the passage of this act, they shall be viewed and treated as intruders in the same manner as those who may become emigrants hereafter.

Be it further Resolved, That the Principal Chief of the Nation be, and he is hereby authorized, by and with the advice of the executive councillors[sic], to order the apprehension of any intruders within the limits of the Nation, to be delivered over to the agent of the United States for the Cherokees, to be prosecuted under the intercourse laws of the United States, or to expel or punish them as they please.

Approved: JOHN ROSS,
Principal Chief, Cherokee Nation.
New Echota, October 31, 1829.

Louisiana was delivered to the United States at St. Louis on March 10, 1804, and all of that portion lying north of the thirty-fifth parallel was constituted, on March 3, 1805, the Territory of Louisiana.

During the month of December, 1811, the great siesmatic disturbances of the St. Francis River country, in which the Cherokees were located, caused much of this territory to be submerged, and many of the Cherokees, fearing that this community was under the ban of the Great Spirit, moved enmass to a new location between the Arkansas and White rivers.*

On June 4, 1812, the Congress of the United States created the Territory of Missouri, and on the succeeding December 31st, the county of Arkansas, Territory of Missouri, was created, embracing practically the present State of Arkansas; and during the following year Lawrence County was constituted from that portion of Arkansas County lying north of the mouth of Little Red River. Thus it will be seen that the Cherokee settlement was successively within the Spanish province of Louisiana, Territory of Louisiana, Territory of Missouri and the organized counties of Arkansas and Lawrence, Territory of Missouri. During all of which time they had been settlers without warrant of title to their habitations, and it was not until the ratification of the United States-Cherokee treaty of July 8th, 1817, that they were confirmed in their rights to their homes.

The rights of the "Western Cherokees" to their lands in Arkansas was confirmed by the treaty of 1817, as follows:

"Article 5. The United States binds themselves to exchange for the lands ceded in the first and second articles hereof, to give to that part of the Cherokee Nation on the Arkansas, as much land on said river and White River as they have or may hereafter receive from the Cherokee Nation, east of the Mississippi, acre for acre, as the just proportion due that part of the Nation on the Arkansas, agreeable to their numbers; which is to commence on the north side of the Arkansas River, at the mouth of Point Remove, of Budwell's Old Place; thence, by a straight line, northwardly to strike Chatooga Mountain, or the hill first above Shield's Ferry, on White River, thence running up and between said rivers for complement, the banks of which rivers to be the lines; and to have the above line, from the point of beginning to the point on White River, run and marked; and all citizens of the United States, except Mrs.

---

* State Papers, Indian Affairs, Vol. 11, page 11.

(Persis) Lovely, who is to remain where she lives during life, removed from within the bounds as above named."

In the spring of 1819 Thomas Nuttall, the naturalist, ascended Arkansas River, and gave the following interesting sketch of the Western Cherokees as he found them: "Both banks of the river as we proceeded were lined with the houses and fences of the Cherokees, and although their dress was of a mixture of indigenous and European taste, yet in their houses, which were decently furnished, and in their farms, which were well fenced and stocked, we perceived a happy approach towards civilization. Their numerous families, also well fed and clothed, argue a propitious progress in their population. Their superior industry, either as hunters or farmers, proves the value of property among them, and they are no longer strangers to avarice and the distinctions created by wealth. Some of them are possessed of property to the amount of many thousands of dollars, have houses handsomely and conveniently furnished, and their tables are spread with our dainties and luxuries."

The boundary lines of the "Cherokee Nation West" were run in the spring of 1819 by William Rector, Surveyor General of Arkansas, and was accepted as correct by Reuben Lewis, United States Agent for the Western Cherokees. At that time the Cherokee Agency was at the mouth of Illinois Creek (now Pope County, Arkansas).

Bowl's village was between Shoal and Petit Jean Creeks, on the south side of Arkansas River, and consequently not within the territory ceded to the Cherokees by the treaty of 1817. On account of this fact, and also to gratify a general wish to his townsmen to locate within Spanish territory, he, with sixty of his men and their families, emigrated in the winter of 1819-20 to territory promised them by the Spanish authorities, on the Sabine and Neches Rivers, in the Mexican province of Texas.*

By an act of a Council, held on September 11th, 1821, it was provided that the Western Cherokee Nation should have three chiefs, designated as the First Chief, Second Chief and Third Chief. The First and Second Chiefs were to have an annual salary of one hundred dollars each and the Third Chief was to have an annual salary of sixty dollars. Their tenure of office was to be for four years.

The Nation was divided into four districts, but unfortunately

---

* National Intelligencer, September 15, 1820.

their boundaries and names have not been preserved.

The capital of the Cherokee Nation West from 1813 to 1824 was at Takatoka's Village, and from 1821 to 1828 was Piney, on Piney Creek.

The First Chief of the Western Cherokees was, consecutively: Bowl, 1795-1813; Takatoka, 1813 to 1818; Tahlonteeskee, John Jolly, John Brown and John Rogers. (The latter was deposed and his valuable property was confiscated by Chief John Ross. John Rogers was the grandfather of Chief William C. Rogers.)

The Western Cherokees were in a constant war with the Osages until 1821 or 1822, and for that reason it was necessary to elect three chiefs so as to preserve their executive line of succession, even though the First and Second Chiefs might die or be killed.

For the purpose of holding elections, before 1831, all of the voters were notified to meet at a certain place and time. A couple or more of their leading men would each announce in a tone that could be easily heard the name of his favorite candidate. Each nominator then called on his candidate to follow him and he led him beyond the sight and hearing of the voters, where he left him and returned to the crowd, where he in a short speech outlined the virtues and qualifications of his candidate. Each nominator then stepped off a few steps from the crowd and called for those who preferred his candidate to join him. The nominators then proceeded to an audible count of their partisans. Each group being widely separated from the others, no controversy arose and if there were more than two candidates, the one having the smallest number was dropped and the others balloted on, until someone had received a majority. The candidates were then brought back and the election was proclaimed.

After 1831 the elections were held on the second Monday in July of even numbered years, at the regularly designated precincts of each of the four districts. Each voter stated his preferences and written records of the same were transmitted to Council, and the district judges issued certificates of election to the officers elected by and for the district; but the council counted the votes and declared the election of the chiefs.

By the provisions of a treaty between the United States and the Osage Indians of June 2nd, 1825, the latter ceded to the United States all of their land lying "east of a line to be drawn from the head sources of the Kansas (River) southwardly through the Rock Saline." This was afterwards marked as the hundredth meridian, this becoming automatically the western boundary line of Arkansas.

Lovely County,[†] Arkansas, was created by an act of legislature on October 13th, 1827, embracing all of the land lying west of Pulaski, Arkansas and Lawrence Counties, south of a direct line west from the north boundary line of Arkansas Territory to a point forty miles west of the former northwest corner of said territory, thence in a line directly south to Red River.

A townsite was laid off by John Nicks, on the site of the present Dwight Mission,[*] on Sallisaw Creek. This town was named Nicksville, and was the county seat of Lovely County. James Woodson Bates was appointed judge; Thomas Moore, sheriff, and John Dillard, clerk. Only one term of court was held in this county, as it was abolished by the Arkansas Legislature on October 17th, 1828.

The cause of the extinguishment of Lovely County was that on May 28th, 1828, a treaty between the United States and the Cherokee Nation "West" was ratified by the Congress of the United States. This treaty to Article 4 was as follows:

"Whereas, it being the anxious desire of the Government of the United States to secure to the Cherokee Indians, as well as those now living within the limits of the territory of Arkansas, as those of their friends and brothers who reside in the states east of the Mississippi, and who may wish to join their brothers in the west, a permanent home, and which shall, under the most solemn guarantee of the United States, be and remain theirs forever—a home that shall never, in all future time, be embarrassed by having extended around it the lines, or placed over it the jurisdiction of a territory or state, nor be pressed upon by the extension, in any way, of any of the limits of any existing territory or states; and

"Whereas, The present location of the Cherokees in Arkansas being unfavorable to the present repose, and tending as the past demonstrates, to their further degradation and misery; and the Cherokees being anxious to avoid such consequences, and yet not questioning their rights to their lands in Arkansas, as secured to them by treaty, and resting upon the pledges given them by the President of the United States and the Secretary of War, of March, 1818, and 8th of October, 1821, in

---

[†] Named in honor of William L. Lovely.
[*] In Section 34, Township 13 North, Range 23 East, in Oklahoma.

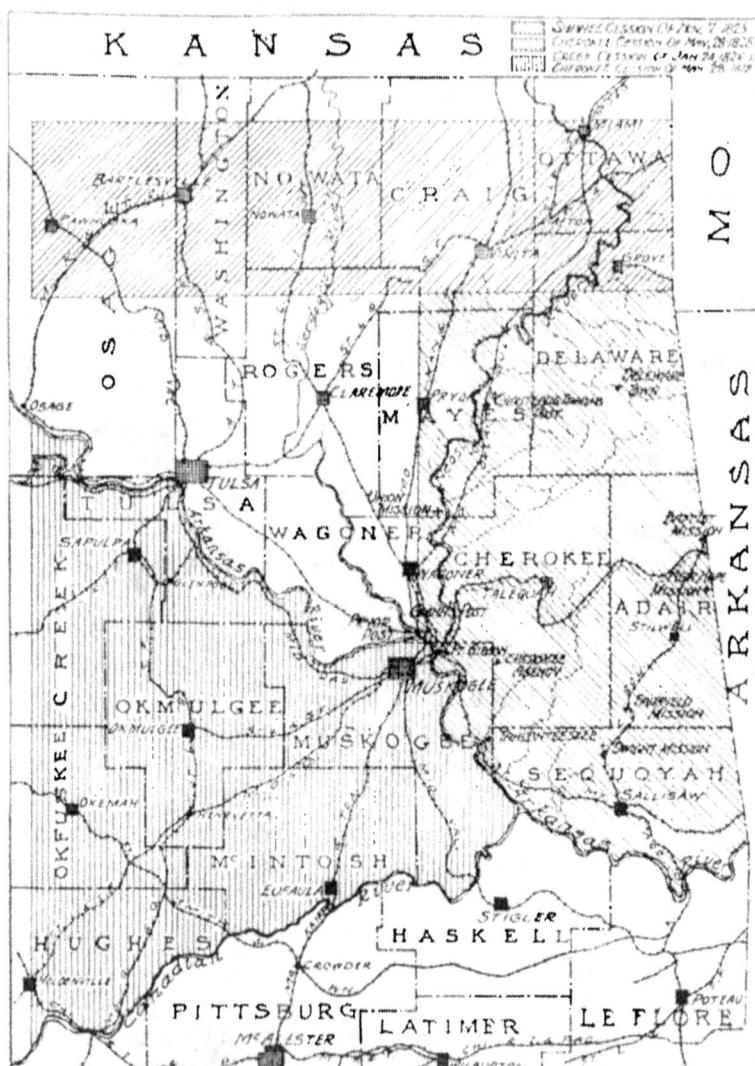

Map of the Western Cherokee Nation from 1828 to December 29, 1832.

regard to the outlet to the West,[*] and as may be seen on referring to the records of the War Department, still anxious to secure a permanent home, and to free themselves and their posterity from an embarrassing connection of the Territory of Arkansas, and guard themselves from such connection in future; and

"Whereas, It being important not to the Cherokees only, but also to the Choctaws, and in regard also to the question which may be agitated in the future respecting the location of the latter, as well as the former, within the limits of the Territory or State of Arkansas, as the case may be, and their removal therefrom; and to avoid the cost which may tend negotiations to rid the Territory or State of Arkansas, whenever it may become a State, of either, or both of those tribes, the parties hereto do hereby conclude the following article, viz:

"Article 1. The western boundary of Arkansas shall be, and the same is hereby, defined, via: A line shall be run, commencing on Red River at a point where the eastern Choctaw line strikes said river, and run due north with said line to the River Arkansas, thence in a direct line to the southwest corner of Missouri.

"Article 2. The United States agrees to possess the Cherokees and to guarantee it to them forever, and that guarantee is hereby solemnly pledged, of seven millions of acres of land, to be bounded as follows, viz: Commencing at that point on Arkansas River where the eastern Choctaw boundary line strikes said river, and running thence with the western line of Arkansas, as defined in the foregoing article, to the southwest corner of Missouri, and thence with the western boundary line of Missouri till it crosses the waters of Neosho, generally called Grand River, thence due west to a point from which a due south course will strike the present northwest corner of Arkansas Territory, thence continuing due south, on and with the present western boundary line of the Territory to the main branch of Arkansas River, thence down said river to its junction with the Canadian River, and thence up and between said Rivers Arkansas and Canadian to a point at which a line running

---

[*] Letter of the Secretary of War, on July 22, 1818, to Reuben Lewis, United States Indian Agent for the Western Cherokees.

Statement of the Secretary of War to the Arkansas Cherokee delegation in Washington, October 8th, 1821.

north and south from river to river will give the aforesaid seven millions of acres. In addition to the seven millions of acres thus provided for and bounded, the United States further guarantee to the Cherokee Nation a perpetual outlet, west, and a free and unmolested use of all the country west of the western boundary of the above described limits, and as far west as the sovereignty of the United States and their right of soil extend.

"Article 3. The United States agrees to have the lines of the above cession run without delay, say not later than the first of October next, and to remove immediately after the running of the eastern line from the Arkansas River to the southwest corner of Missouri, all white persons from the west to the east side of said line, and also all others, should there by[sic] any there, who may be unacceptable to the Cherokees, so that no obstacles arising out of a presence of a white population, or a population of any other sort, shall exist to annoy the Cherokees—and also to keep all such from the west of said line in future."

Pursuant to this treaty the "Western Cherokees" moved to their newly acquired country in 1828-29.

The Cherokees established their capitol at Tahlonteeskee, on Deep Creek (in what is now section 16, township 12 north, range 21 east, ok Oklahoma) and divided their territory into four district, as follows: Lee's Creek, with its courthouse at Little Charles's on Skin Bayou; Sallisaw, with its courthouse at Fox's on Sallisaw Creek; Illinois, with its courthouse at Tahlonteeskee, and Neosho, with its courthouse at John Drew's on Bayou Menard.

On account of the fact that Neosho River did not cross the western boundary line of Missouri as mentioned in the second article of the treaty of 1828 it would have been impossible to mark the northern boundary line of the Cherokee cession had it not been already definitely fixed by the United States-Shawnee treaty of November 7th, 1825, the granting clause of which read as follows: "Article 2. It is further agreed by the contracting parties that, in consideration of the cession aforesaid, the United States do hereby agree to give to the Shawnee tribe of Indians, within the State of Missouri, for themselves and for those of the same nation now residing in Ohio, who may hereafter emigrate to the west of the Mississippi, a tract of land equal to fifty (50) miles square, situated west of the State of Missouri, and within the purchase lately made from the Osages, by the treaty bearing date the second day of June, one thousand eight hundred and twenty-five; and within the following boundaries: Commencing at a point two (2) miles northwest of the southwest corner of the State of Missouri, from thence north twenty-five (25) miles, thence west one hundred (100) miles, thence south twenty-five (25) miles, thence east one hundred (100) miles to the place of beginning."*

The western boundaries were complicated in the same way on account of the fact that under the treaties of 1826-27 the Muskogee Indians had selected lands between the Canadian and Arkansas Rivers. Cherokees and Muskogees had settled on the land laying between the Arkansas and Canadian Rivers, and serious disputes arose between them as to who owned the land. To secure peace, representatives of the United States Government induced delegations from both of these tribes to assemble at Fort Gibson, where, on the fourteenth day of February, 1833, separate treaties were concluded with them whereby their lines were more definitely fixed.

From 1835 to 1838, "Eastern" Cherokees of the "Treaty Party" emigrated west and became incorporated in friendly affiliation with the "Western" Cherokees.

The United States had a survey made of the boundaries of the "Western" Cherokee Nation in 1837. This was done under the supervision of Reverend Isaac McCoy.*

A majority of the Cherokee Nation, residing east of the Mississippi had been, and continued unalterably, opposed to the terms of the treaty of 1817. This difference of sentiment upon a subject so vital to their welfare was productive of much bitterness and violent animosities. Those who had favored the emigration or had been induced, either through personal preference or by the subsidizing influences of the Government agents, to favor the conclusion of the treaty, became the

---

* United States Statutes at Large, Vol. VII, page 284.
* Senate Document 120, 25th Congress, 2nd Session, page 954.

Thomas Mitchell Buffington. Cherokee genealogy No. $1^1 1^2 1^3 7^4 2^5 7^6$. Principal Chief of the Cherokee Nation from November, 1899, to November, 1903.

objects of scorn and hatred of the remainder of the Nation; they were made the subjects of a persecution so relentless, while they remained in the "Eastern" country, that it was never forgotten, and, when in the course of events, the remainder of the tribe was forced to remove to the country west of the Mississippi and join the earlier emigrants and the "Old Settlers," the old dissentions broke out afresh, and on these lines the earlier political parties were based, and to the end of their tribal existence the fundamental basis of the two political parties could be traced to this then obscure source.

As instances of the variance of statements in regard to the habitability of the "Western Country," I will append a letter written by John Ridge and a poem written by John Howard Payne, who was at that time in the employ of Chief John Ross, as a publicity agent.

Ridge's letter was as follows:

South Lee, Berkshire County, Mass.
May 7th, 1838.

"My Dear Friend:

"While I was in New York I received your kind letter of the 24th ult., in answer to mine, for which I am greatly indebted to you. It was my desire to have visited Washington, in order to have had the pleasure of a personal interview with you, and also to have seen the result of the great Indian bill, now in a course of discussion in the Senate. But the period I have set apart to return to my country is the first of June, and I have but a short time to spend amongst my wife's relations. I did not write as fully as the interesting subject of Cherokee removal and the nature of the country demanded, as I then believed that I should see you.

"Now, you will allow me to relate my opinion of our country in the West, and the situation of our people. The Treaty is so liberal in its provisions for the comfortable removal of the Cherokees that I have heard no complaint on that head, but the highest satisfaction. Those who went by water, by steamboats, in the spring of the year, passed with so much dispatch that the most of them planted corn and raised considerable crops. You know that good and exemplary Christian, Mr. Charles Moore. He said that he planted in the month of June and raised a greater crop of beans, pumpkins and corn than he ever did in Georgia, under the most favorable circumstances. He said that the land in the West was so rich that he could compare it to nothing else but a fattened hog, which was so fat that he could not get up. I have traveled extensively in that country—once from my residence, near the Missouri and Arkansas corner, to Fort Smith, through Flint district, where I had the pleasure of beholding fine springs of water, excellent farms and comfortable houses and mills and mission schools, belonging to the Cherokees, and every evidence of prosperity and happiness was to be seen among the Cherokees as a people. I saw a number who had previously arrived, and had arrived since I had, and I heard but one sentiment—that they were happy and contented in their new country. Indeed, the soil is exceedingly rich and well timbered, and the navigation of the Arkansas River affords them superior commercial advantages to what they enjoyed in the East. I joked with the people, and asked them if they wished to return to Georgia, even if they could be re-established in their ancient rights and locations in that country. They invariably said, 'No; by no means. Nothing would induce them to return.' But they sincerely wished that the eyes of their countrymen might be opened, and break from the delusions of John Ross and his political tools and escape to this good land. I think in this direction I traveled over eighty-eight miles, in a straight direction. After this, I visited the newly acquired land, called Neutral Ground, which was added to our country, west, by the Treaty of New Echota. I rode over it, about two days, and I there found Mr. Joseph Rogers, our Cherokee friend, from the Chattahoochie, pleasantly situated in the finest region of country I ever beheld in any part of the United States.

"The streams here, of all sizes, from the rivers to the brooks, run swiftly over clear stones and pebbles, and the water is as clear as crystal, in which excellent fish abound in vast numbers. The soil is diversified from the best prairie lands to the best bottom lands, in vast tracts. Never did I see a better location for settlements and better springs in the world. God has thrown His favors here with a broad cast. In this region are numerous mills, and it is of itself capable of supporting a larger population than the whole Cherokee Nation, East. On my return, I traveled toward Fort Gibson, seventy-five miles in another direction, and I found the richness of the soil and natural advantages far superior to any country which I had seen in all my travel. In this trip I visited Park Hill

Mission, where the Reverend Mr. Worcester and Mr. Boudinot are located, and are engaged in the translation and publication of useful religious books in the Cherokee language, and also Choctaw books, prepared by the Choctaw missionaries.

"But what pleased me more, and was a new thing here in this country, those gentlemen had published a Christian almanac,* in Cherokee and English, calculated for the meridian of Fort Gibson. I found this extensively in circulation amongst the Cherokees, and, in fact, I was pleased to find religious tracts, in the Indian language, were on the shelves of full blood Cherokees, and every one knew and seemed to love the Messenger, as they call Mr. Worcester. I very often met with new emigrants from the Eastern Nation, either arriving or settling the country, or on their way to Fort Gibson, to draw the balance of their dues for their lands and improvements. These newcomers were formerly of opposite parties in the old Nation. There was no disposition to quarrel, but every disposition manifested to cultivate friendship and rejoice together in the possession of this fine country.

"I had the pleasure of being introduced to General Arbuckle, commanding at Fort Gibson,† and I found him to be an excellent man, of fine personal appearance and intelligent. He informed me that the country next to the Osages, on the Verdigris, was the best in the country, and was yet unsettled; so you perceive that I am greatly pleased with our new country. Most all the intelligent men of our Nation, our Supreme Judges and Sheriffs and Marshals, our Legislators and our National Treasurer, are, you are aware, already removed, and are engaged in the building of houses and the opening of farms. Many of the Cherokees have turned their attention to merchandising, and some have supplied themselves with goods from New Orleans and New York, besides other places more convenient to the Nation.

"Many of the Christian Cherokees are engaged in the organization of schools and temperance societies, and there is no danger, as some supposed, that the Cherokees would retrograde and turn to the chase, instead of the pursuits of civilization. And I have the pleasure also of informing you that the utmost friendship and tranquility prevails

---

* The Cherokee Almanac was published for each of the years from 1836 to 1861, with the possible exception of one for the year 1837.
† Fort Gibson was established in 1824.

between the Indians and the citizens of the United States, not only those who live at the military stations, but those of your citizens that reside in Missouri and Arkansas, near the Cherokee Nation.

"In the best state of friendship they visit and trade together, on both sides of the line, to their mutual advantage. In addition to this, we have some excellent saline springs, where salt is made by the Cherokees. I was told that Judge Martin* was about to commence work at one of these salines. In regard to the health of the country, I find it good, on the small waters, and it is only on the larger water courses that the fever and ague prevails among the new settlers. But it is somewhat singular that whenever a Cherokee arrives in the country, wherever that may be, he cannot be induced to change his location for a better. He will either say there is no better, or that it is a good as we wants[sic] it to be.

"If the people of the United States could only see our condition in the West, they would no longer assist John Ross to delude the poor, ignorant portion of our people to remain in the East, where he can speculate on their miseries.

"The Cherokee government in the West is very much like it was in the Old Nation, before it was suppressed by the States. They have an executive, legislature and judiciary and trial by jury.

"I feel happy to ascertain that a majority of the Senate of the United States entertain such magnanimous views towards the well being of the Indians in the future, removed as they are from the State jurisdiction and conflict. With the rich advantages of the Christian religion and cultivation, the Choctaws, Cherokees, Chickasaws, Creeks and other Nations are destined to become a great and mighty people in the great West. I am truly pleased to find that our neighbor, Senator Sevier, stands by your side in the great undertaking. That was a happy thought of his calling the Indian Territory 'Neosho.' It means, in the Osage language, the 'Clear Waters.'[†]

"I should be glad to receive the documents connected with that bill, and all the important speeches on the subject.

"While I was in New York, I found that the religious community was entirely bewildered by John Ross and in the partisanship of their

---

* Judge John Martin, 1—$1^1 1^2 3^3 9^4$.

[†] This interpretation is incorrect; Neosho is an Osage word meaning river of ponds or lakes.

papers. Instead of receiving the late treaty as a blessing to the Cherokees, and as a measure of relief to them, they considered it the source of all their afflictions. I attempted to explain John Ross's position in the papers, and many of them are now convinced that the treaty and its friends are in the right; but a great many are still bewildered. They believe that John Ross is the Nation, and, could he succeed in breaking the treaty, that the whole of the Southern States would retire from their jurisdictional charters.

"I sometimes feel afraid that all is not right in these editors of newspapers. It would seem that they would be willing to have the Indians resist and shed blood, and produce a Florida scene, in order to render their Government odious.

"They seem pleased to have money expended to suppress Indian hostilities, and then blame the Government for the expenses. They well know that the Indians cannot exist in the States, and all they can possibly accomplish by heir memorials is to assist John Ross to effect a treaty, the character of which is buried in his breast.

"They all know that in the East the Cherokees have no government, and have had no elections for nine years past; and yet John Ross is, in their estimation, a constitutional chief over all the Cherokees, and if the President refuses to recognize this preposterous claim and determines to see that all the Cherokees shall share alike from the avails of their land, then they proclaim him a monster and John Ross the Cherokee Christian.

"I shall remain here to the first of June, and I shall be obliged to you for another letter before I leave for the West.

I am your friend,
JOHN RIDGE."

To Governor Wilson Lumpkin:[*]

---

[*] Removal of the Cherokee Indians from Georgia, Wilson Lumpkin, Volume 11, page 201.

The Lament of the Cherokee.
By John Howard Payne, author of Home, Sweet Home.

O, soft falls the dew, on the twilight descending,
And tall grows the shadowy hill on the plain;
And night over the distant forest is bending
Like the storm spirit, dark, o'er the tremulous main.

But midnight enshrouded my lone heart in its dwelling,
A tumult of woe in my bosom is swelling
And a year unbefitting the warrior is telling
That hope has abandoned the brave Cherokee.

Can a tree that is torn from its root by the fountain,
The price of the valley; green, spreading and fair,
Can it flourish, removed to the rock of the mountain,
Unwarmed by the sun and unwatered by care?

Though vesper be kind, her sweet dews in bestowing,
No life giving brook in its shadows is flowing,
And when the chill winds of the desert are blowing.
So droops the transplanted and lone Cherokee.

Sacred graves of my sires; have I left you forever?
How melted my heart when I bade you adieu;
Shall joy light the face of the Indian? Ah, never;
While memory sad has the power to renew.

As flies the fleet deer when the blood hound is started,
So fled winged hope from the poor broken hearted;
Oh, could she have turned ere forever departing,
And beckoned with smiles to her sad Cherokee.

Is it the low wind through the wet willows rushing,
That fills with wild numbers my listening ear?
Or is it some hermit rill in the solitude gushing,
The strange playing minstrel, whose music I hear?

'Tis the voice of my father, slow, solemnly stealing,
I see his dim form by yon meteor, kneeling
To the God of the White man, the Christian, appealing.
He prays for the foe of the dark Cherokee.

Great Spirit of Good, whose abode is in Heaven,
Whose wampum of peace is the bow in the sky,
Wilt thou give to the wants of the clamorous ravens,
Yet turn a deaf ear to my piteous cry?

O'er the ruins of home, o'er my heart's desolation;
No more shalt thou hear my unblest lamentation;
For death's dark encounter, I make preparation;
He hears the last groan of the wild Cherokee.

LAWS OF THE OLD SETTLER CHEROKEES.

Act Relative to Light-Horse Company.

(Verbal law, printed by request of John Jolly.)
Resolved, That there be and is hereby appointed a Light-Horse company whose duty shall be to preserve peace and good order among the Cherokees on the Arkansas to suppress stealing, and punish such as may be caught in such act.

Resolved further, That the Light-Horse company shall not have anything to do with a case of stealing, which has been committed previous to this date, neither shall it be lawful for any Light-Horse company hereafter appointed, or Chiefs, to have any cognizance of such cases, (stealing) if committed previous to this date.

Dardanelle Rock, 1820.

JOHN JOLLY, Prin'l. Chief.

Walter Webber, Black Fox, Spring Frog, Too-cho-wuh, and others, Chiefs, Headmen and Warriors of the Cherokee Nation.

Establishing the Executive Department.

On examination the National papers and documents containing the laws of the Cherokee Nation, we find that the first law committed to writing was done at a Council held on Piney Creek at John Smith's house, bearing date of 11th September, 1824, which law or act of said date, refers back to a law passed at a Council held Ta-ka-to-ka's village, Illinois Bayou, A. T., on the 21st of July, 1824, at which time the Nation was divided into four districts, and the people of each district were required to select or appoint two persons out of each one of their respective districts, who were to serve for a term of twelve months, and when convened were to be called the National Committee. Accordingly, the people met in their respective districts and selected their members making in all eight members, which members convened at John Smith's on Piney, Sept. 11th, 1824, as before stated; and after organizing themselves into a committee, Col. Walter Webber was called upon to preside as chairman of the committee, and David Brown appointed clerk, whereupon the National Committee proceeded as follows:*

Resolved by the National Committee, in General Council Convened, That from and after the date of this, the Executive Department of the Cherokee Government shall consist of three persons, that is, a First Chief, a Second Chief, and a Third or minor Chief, which chiefs shall serve for a term of four years from the date of their appointment, and the First and Second Chiefs shall receive a salary of one hundred dollars annually, and the Third or minor Chief, sixty dollars.

By order of the National Committee.

Piney, Sept. 11th, 1824.

Approved—JOHN JOLLY, Prin'l. Chief.

WALTER WEBBER, Chairman.

An Act Relative to Breach of Marriage.

Resolved by the National Committee and Council, in General Council Convened, That it shall be unlawful for a White man, (citizen of

---

* Note to Hercules T. Martin, compiler of laws of the Cherokee Nation, under act of Cherokee National Council, Oct. 30, 1848.

the United States living in the Nation, to have more than one wife; neither shall he make use of the woman's (his wife) property without her consent.

Furthermore, If a White man should leave his wife, without a ust[sic] cause, such White man shall be tried for such act, before the judges, and if convicted, he shall pay the woman left, all damages done her for breach of marriage and for deceiving her. The amount of damages to be decided by the judges.

Piney, Sept. 24, 1824.
Approved.

JOHN JOLLY,
BLACK COAT,
Chiefs.

An Act of Oblivion Between the Seven Clans, Etc.

Resolved by the National Committee and Council, in General Council Convened, That all lives taken, for which the different clans of the Cherokee people are indebted to each other for lives taken previous to this date, shall be, and are hereby forgiven; and all such claims for life taken as above stated, heretofore existing between the said different clans, and up to the present time, shall cease to exist, and be forever forgotten, and suffered to pass out of remembrance.

Piney, Sept. 24th, 1824.

WALTER WEBBER, Chairman.
Approved: —JOHN JOLLY.

An Act Relative to Casual Deaths.

Resolved by the National Committee and Council, in General Council Convened, That hereafter if it should so happen, that one or more persons should accidentally, and without malice or revenge, kill or cause the death of one or more persons, the case shall be tried before the judges of the district where the circumstances took place, or by the National Council, and if it should be proven satisfactory, before either of the said authorities, that the cause of such person or persons' deaths was

117

by accident, and without malice or revenge, the person or persons arranged to trial, and thus cleared of being guilty of murder shall be acquitted and set at liberty.

Piney, Sept. 24th, 1824.

Approved—JOHN JOLLY, Prin'l. Chief.

An Act Relating to the National Council and Members.

Resolved by the Committee and Council, in General Council Convened, That the law heretofore in force, requiring the National Council to commence annually, on the first Monday in September, be, and is hereby repealed, and in lieu thereof,

Resolved, That from and after this date, the annual National Council shall commence on the first Monday in October, annually, which shall be held at Tah-lon-tee-skee Council House, Cherokee Nation.

Resolved Further, That from and after this date, each member of the National Committee and Council, and clerks of each house, shall be and are hereby required to be present at Tah-lon-tee-skee Council House, annually, by 10 o'clock a. m., on the day set forth by law for the annual National Council to commence. And also, if the chiefs should call a place and time for the National Council to meet, they (the members and clerks) shall be present at the place appointed by 10 o'clock a. m., on the day set forth by the chiefs for the Council to meet. And any member or members, or clerks of the National Council, failing to attend an annual National Council or a call Council, at the time and place as above required, shall be subject to and forfeit a fine of five dollars each per day, for each and every day such member or members, or clerks, are absent; which fine shall be paid into the National Treasury. But in case any such member or clerk shall be unable to attend as above required, on account of their being sick, or any of their family, or if they have any other justifiable cause or detention for non-attendance, they shall then be exempt from fine, but shall in such cases, inform the council then in session, of their situation, otherwise the fine may stand open against them.

Approved—JOHN JOLLY, Prin'l. Chief.

O. H. P. Brewer. Cherokee genealogy No. III—$1^1 1^2 3^3 1^4 2^5 1^6 5^7$.
Cherokee Senator. President of the Cherokee Board of Education
and Member of the Oklahoma State Constitutional Convention.
Present Postmaster of Muskogee.

An Act Relative to Abandoned Improvements.

Resolved by the Committee and Council, in General Council Convened, That from and after this date, all improvements with the Cherokee Nation, such as fencing, cleared lands, and buildings of any description, and which have been made or caused to be made, or improved by United States license traders, or by White intruders, shall, when abandoned, or intruders removed therefrom, revert to the Cherokee Nation.

Resolved further, That it is hereby enjoined as a duty upon the judges of the same district where such improvements may be, to make sale of them as herein stated; that is, the judge as above stated shall repair to the place where such improvements are and take a minute description of them and publish the same for four or six months, at two or more public places in the nation, notifying in the advertisement that at the expiration of such time the improvements or buildings as the case may be, thus advertised, will be sold to the highest bidder, at public auction on a twelve months' credit, and that the purchaser will be required to give bond and good security for the purchase money. Accordingly, at the expiration of said time (four or six months) the judges shall repair to the improvement advertised, or to a more suitable place, and make sale of it as mentioned in the advertisement, and procure from the purchaser a bond for double the amount of the purchase money, with approved security attached thereto, which bond shall be drawn payable in twelve months from the date of purchase, and made payable to the national council or chiefs for the benefit of the nation; and at the next ensuing national council thereafter, all such bonds shall be handed into the national council. And after such sale has been effected the judges and light-horse will see that the purchaser under the law gets peaceable possession of the improvement purchased.

Resolved further, That all improvements or buildings which may revert to the nation by the foregoing resolution, from and after this date shall not be taken possession of or meddled with by any person or persons in any way whatever, unless they shall have first obtained a right by purchase under the law, and if any person or persons should disregard this law and proceed to a violation, he, she or they shall be subject to and forfeit a fine at the discretion of the national council.

Tah-lon-tee-skee, March 2d, 1831.
Approved—JOHN JOLLY, Prin'l. Chief.

___

Resolution Allowing the Light-Horse to Defend Themselves.
Resolved by the national Committee and Council, in General Council Convened, That if any person or persons should raise a weapon against one or more of the national light-horse while in the exercise of their duty, they shall be, and are hereby made justifiable in such case to defend themselves; and if any one or more of the light-horse should kill such person or persons, so raising a weapon, he or they (the light-horse) shall not be accounted guilty of murder.
Tah-lon-tee-skee, March 20, 1831.
Approved—JOHN JOLLY.

___

An Act, Granting a Person Convicted of Theft to Make an Appeal.
Resolved, by the National Committee and Council, in General Council Convened, That if any person or persons should be convicted of theft, before the district judges, and such person or persons, so convicted, believes that they have been unjustly convicted, they shall have a right to demand an appeal to the national council for a new trial, and the judges before whom the case was tried, are hereby required to grant such convicts an appeal; —provided the convict can make it appear to the judged, that he, she or they, had not at that time a fair and full trial; and in case an appeal is granted, under the foregoing circumstances, the person or persons obtaining such an appeal, shall be required to give bond for double the amount of the property alleged to have been stolen, and also to give good security for their appearance at the ensuing national council thereafter. But in case such bond and security is not given, an appeal shall not be granted.
Tah-lon-tee-skee, March 21, 1831.
Approved—JOHN JOLLY.

An Act, Relative to the Duties of the National Light-Horse.

Resolved by the National Committee and Council, in General Council Convened, That the national light-horse of each district in the Cherokee nation, shall be, and they are hereby required to be present and attend all national councils, provided they are able and have no duties to attend to in their districts, during the session of the national council; whose duty it shall be to preserve peace and good order at and about the council, during its session.

Resolved, further, That it shall be the duty of the national light-horse, to suppress stealing, breaking open and burning houses, and to bring criminals and offenders of the law to justice, and to protect orphans and their property, and to execute the decision of the judges when required.

Resolved, further, That it shall be the duty of the light-horse to collect debts, or accounts; provided, such debts or accounts are disputed by the debtor, and afterwards proved by the creditor before one or more of the district judges to be just, in which case the light-horse can proceed to collect, and demand, ten per cent for collection off the debtor.

Further resolved by the National Committee and Council, in General Council Convened, That if the national light-horse should have a horse to die from under them, while on duty, such horse shall be appraised by two good disinterested men, for what such horse was worth, before he died, and the owner shall be required to obtain a certificate of the amount of such appraisement, from under the hands of the appraisers, which shall be a voucher of such appraisement; and if the national council is satisfied, that such horse did die, while on duty, the amount thereof shall be paid out of the national annuity or other national funds. But if such horse should die, while returning from off of duty, then the nation shall be exempt from payment.

Tah-lon-tee-skee, March 21, 1831.

Approved—JOHN JOLLY.

An Act for the Punishment of Criminal Offenses.

Resolved by the National Committee and Council, in General Council Convened, That where a part of the penalty under the law for a

Charles D. Carter. Cherokee genealogy No. IV—$1^1 3^2 4^3 2^4$.
Member of Congress from the Third and Second Districts of
Oklahoma from 1907 until the present time.

crime is punishment by whipping, such punishment shall be inflicted by the light-horse, and the number of stripes or lashes to be received by criminals shall be from twenty-five to sixty, neither more nor less, but to be regulated as the judges may decide according to the magnitude of the crime committed.

Resolved, Further, That whosoever shall be guilty of theft, robbery, breaking open or burning houses, or of committing a rape upon a female, shall be tried before the judges of the district where the offense was committed, and if convicted of either of the above offenses by good evidence, such person or persons so convicted, shall suffer the penalty of the law by receiving as many lashes on the bare back as the judges may decide, and also such convicts shall make whole the property destroyed, or damages done the injured person, or if for theft, the property stolen shall be returned to the person from who it was taken.

Tah-lon-tee-skee, March 21, 1831.

Approved—JOHN JOLLY.

An Act Prohibiting the Cutting Down of Pecan Trees and Setting the Woods on Fire.

Resolved by the Committee and Council, in General Council Convened, That from and after this date it shall be unlawful for any person or persons to cut down or fell a pecan tree or trees barely for the purpose of obtaining the pecans on such trees; and any person or persons violating this law shall be tried before the judged of the district where the offense was committed, and if convicted, he, she or they so convicted shall pay for each and every such offense five dollars, one-half to be paid to the informer and the other half to the light-horse arraigning such offenders to trial.

And it shall be unlawful for any person or persons to set the woods on fire within the limits of the Cherokee nation before the first of March in each year, from and after this date, and any person violating this law shall be tried before the judges of the district where the offense was committed, and if convicted they shall pay a fine of five dollars for each and every offense, and pay for all damages done by the fire so set out, one-half of the fine to belong to the informer and the other half to the light-horse.

And the national light-horse of each district shall have cognizance of each of the above offenses.

Tah-lon-tee-skee, March 22, 1831.

Approved—JOHN JOLLY.

An Act Prohibiting the Sale of Land, Etc.

Resolved by the National Committee and Council, in General Council Convened, That if any person or persons should sell or bargain the land of the Cherokee Nation, or any part thereof, to a different Nation, or to any person or persons without proper authority from the National Council, and the same approved of by the Chiefs of the Cherokee Nation, they (the offenders), shall be tried for each and every such offense before the National Council, and if convicted by good evidence, such offender or offenders shall suffer death; but if detected before they have actually sold the land, then the punishment shall be one hundred lashes on the bare back, to be inflicted by the National Light-horse. All laws to the contrary notwithstanding.

Resolved Further, That is any person or persons should endeavor to cause the lands of the Cherokee Nation to be laid off into sections, or to make division in it, or meddle themselves in such a way, or in any manner, whatever with the land, without proper authority from the National Council, and the same approved of by the Chiefs of the Cherokee Nation, such person or persons, shall, on conviction, before the National Council, receive one hundred lashes on the bare back, to be inflicted by the National Light-horse. All laws to the contrary notwithstanding.

Tah-lon-tee-skee, March 23, 1831.

Approved—JOHN JOLLY.

An Act Prohibiting White Men Cutting Timber.

Resolved by the National Committee and Council, in General Council Convened, That from and after this date, it shall be unlawful for any person or persons, living in the Nation, to authorize a white man or men, in any shape or manner whatever, to cut lumber or timber upon the

125

lands of the Cherokee Nation, for the use of a white man or men, living out of the Nation. And any person or persons living in the Cherokee Nation, violating this law, shall, on being convicted for such offense, before the Judges of the District where the offense was committed, pay a fine of fifty dollars for each and every such offense, for the benefit of the Nation; or if any person or persons, living in the Nation, should hire to cut lumber or timber, on the lands of the Nation, they shall pay a fine of fifty dollars. Citizens of the Nation are not prevented by this law, from cutting cord-wood for steamboats.

Tah-lon-tee-skee, March 23, 1831.

Approved—JOHN JOLLY.

An Act Confirming Former Decisions.

Resolved by the Nation[sic] Committee and Council, in General Council Convened, That from and after this date, all decisions of the Committee and Council or Light-horse companies, or Chiefs in Council, shall be final and conclusive. And the Committee and council, Judges and Light-horse companies, shall have no cognizance of such cases that have transpired previous to this date, under the then existing law and customs of the Cherokees. This law shall not be so construed, as to prevent the investigation of any due bills that may have been illegally issued by the National authorities.

Tah-lon-tee-skee, March 23, 1831.

Approved—JOHN JOLLY.

An Act Defining Lawful Fences.

Resolved by the National Committee and Council, in General Council Convened, That all persons having farms or other enclosures within the limits of the Cherokee Nation, are hereby required to have a fence of nine good rails high, and the cracks in the fence within the space of two feet from the ground up, not to exceed four inches in width. And all fences filling this description, shall be considered lawful fences, and all as falls short of it, shall be without the law's protection. And should stock of any kind break into or over a lawful fence, the damages shall be estimated by two good disinterested men; and the owner of such stock shall pay the person injured, the amount of such estimation of damages, and the person injured must notify the owner of the stock to come and take it away.

Resolved Further, That if stock of any kind (horses, cattle and hogs) should break into or over an unlawful fence and the owner of the fence should kill or cause to be killed, or injure such stock, he, she or they, shall be accountable to the owner of the stock for all damages done it.

Tah-lon-tee-skee, March 23, 1831.

Approved—JOHN JOLLY.

An Act Relative to Stray Property.

Resolved by the Committee and Council, in General Council Convened, That it shall be the duty of the National Light-horse, to take up all stray property, such as horses, cattle and hogs, which they may find in their respective Districts, and to put the same into good, honest, and careful hands for safe keeping, until the expiration of six months, as set forth by law, hereafter expressed, unless an owner should prove it away under the law in a shorter time.

Further Resolved, That such persons as have charge of stray stock, under the law, shall be allowed for their trouble of keeping it, fifty cents per week for each horse, and fifty cents per month for each head of cattle, and twenty-five cents per month for each hog, which charges are to be paid according to the time the stock is in charge, and to be paid by the owner, before taking the stock out of the hands of the keeper, which charges may be paid in trade, or cash, as the owner wishes. But in case no owner should come forward for such property, until the expiration of six months, and it should be sold as the law hereafter directs, at public auction, for the benefit of the Nation, then the keeper shall have recourse on the Nation, (National Council) for their charges, payable out of the sale money of such stock when collected; but the keeper in such case shall be required to obtain from under the hands of the Light-horse a certified account of their charges, which shall be a voucher to the National Council for the true amount due for keeping.

Resolved Further, That it shall be the duty of the National Light-horse, after taking up and putting in care stray stock, as hereinbefore required, to advertise such stock for six months at two or more public places in their respective Districts, setting forth in the advertisement, the kind of stock, and giving a full description of it, and otherwise, at the expiration of the six months, from the date of the advertisements, such stock will be sold at public auction, for the benefit of the Cherokee Nation.

Furthermore, The Light-horse advertising such property, are hereby required to transmit a copy of the same to the Light-horse in each of the other districts, whose duty shall be to advertise the same also for six months, in their respective Districts, and likewise a copy of the advertisement must be recorded in the District Judge's office, where the property was taken up, and another copy must be transmitted to the United States Agent.

Resolved Further, That the National Light-horse shall be entitled to, for taking up and advertising stray stock, as the law directs fifty cents per head for cattle, and one dollar per head for horses, and twenty-five cents per head for hogs, to be paid by the owner, or the Nation, as the case may be.

Resolved Further, That if any person or persons, should assume a claim to stray property, which is taken up and advertised as the law requires, before the expiration of six months, as set forth in the advertisement, and the said claimant proves before the district judges to the satisfaction of the Light-horse, who took up and advertised the property, that the property advertised is their property, (claimants), then the National Light-horse shall put such claimant in possession of the property proved, after the charges for keeping and advertising have been satisfied.

Resolved Further, That all stray property, such as horses, cattle and hogs, which is and may be taken up and advertised under the law, and no owner, for such stock appearing until the expiration of six months, as set forth in the advertisement; all such stock so advertised shall be immediately sold by the National Light-horse at public auction, to the highest bidder, on a credit of twelve months, for the benefit of the Nation. And the Light-horse who sell such property under the law, shall cause the purchaser to execute a bond for double the amount of the purchase money, and also to give good security for the sure payment of the same when due, which bonds shall be in such case, drawn payable to the National Council for the benefit of the Cherokee Nation. And all purchasers of such property, under the law, shall be, and are hereby bound to keep such property, so purchased twelve months from the time of purchasing it under the law; and in case an owner should come within the said time, (12 months) and prove as before stated to the satisfaction of the Light-horse, that such property so sold was his or theirs; then the Light-horse, shall put the claimant in possession of the property after all charges according to law, have been satisfied—likewise if an owner should prove such property to be his or theirs, after the twelve months run out, then such claimant shall be entitled to four-fifths of the money which it sold for under the law.

Tah-lon-tee-skee, March 24, 1831.

Approved—JOHN JOLLY.

An Act Relative to the Duties of the Judges and Light-horse.

Resolved by the National Committee and Council, in General Council Convened, That it shall be, and is hereby made the duty of the District Judges to act upon all cases laid before them for trial and decision, by the National Light-horse or other citizens of the Cherokee Nation, and to decide upon them agreeable to law and evidence, (that in such cases as come within their jurisdiction, and respective districts); and it is hereby further required, that the Judges in each District shall keep an authentic and correct record of all their decisions upon cases of trial, setting forth the nature of the case decided upon, the evidence proceeded for or against it, and their final decision.

Resolved Further, That where the District Judges are unable to form a decision upon a case, they shall have, hereby, the right to refer the parties concerned in the cases to the National Council for a decision.

Resolved Further, That it shall be the duty of the Judges to superintend the elections held according to law in their respective Districts, and to give each member elected to the National Council, and to each Judge and Light-horse, a certificate, certifying to the National Council, that such members, Judges and Light-horse were truly elected according to law, as set forth in their certificate.

Tah-lon-tee-skee, Sept. 10, 1831.
Approved—JOHN JOLLY,
BLACK COAT,
Chiefs.

_____

An Act Prohibiting the Sale of Ardent Spirits During Council.

Resolved by the National Committee and Council, in General Council Convened, That from and after this date, it shall be unlawful for any person or persons to vend ardent spirits, within five miles of the National Council House, (Tah-lon-tee-skee) during the session of the National; and it shall also be unlawful to vend ardent spirits within five miles of a call Council, during the session, and any person or persons violating (this law inclusive), shall pay a fine of five dollars, for each and every such offense; and the money arising from such fines shall be paid into the National Treasury.

Tah-lon-tee-skee, September 19, 1831.
Approved—JOHN JOLLY.

_____

An Act Authorizing the Light-Horse to Summons Assistance.

Resolved, That where any of the National Light-horse are unable to bring criminals or other persons to justice, they shall be, and are hereby empowered to summons one or two persons and not more to assist them in executing their duties; and the person or persons so summoned shall be entitled to one dollar per day while in service, payable out of the National funds. And the Light-horse shall be, and they are hereby required to give each person so summoned, a certificate to the National Council specifying the time such persons were in service and the amount due. And in case the Light-house[sic] should summons any person or persons to assist them in their duties, and if such person or persons so summoned should refuse to serve, he or they so refusing shall forfeit and pay a fine of five dollars each for the benefit of the Cherokee Nation.

Tah-lon-tee-skee, September 19, 1831.
Approved—JOHN JOLLY, Prin'l. Chief.

Samuel Houston Adopted.

Resolved by the National Committee and Council in General Council Convened, That in consideration of his former acquaintance with, and services rendered to the Cherokees and his present disposition to improve their condition and benefit their circumstances, and our confidence in his integrity and honor, if he should remain among us, we do solemnly, firmly, and irrevocably grant to Samuel Houston forever, all the rights, privileges, and immunities of a citizen of the Cherokee Nation.

WALTER WEBBER,
President of Committee.
WILLIAM THORNTON,
Clerk of Committee.
AARON PRICE,
Speaker of Council.
JOHN BROWN,
Clerk of Council.
Tah-lon-tee-skee, October 31, 1831.*
Approved—JOHN JOLLY.

An Act Imposing a Fine for Harboring Unruly White Men.

Resolved by the National Committee and Council, in General Council Convened, That if any person or persons, should from and after this date, harbor a citizen or citizens of the United States, about their house or other place in the Nation, who have been turned out of the Nation for a crime or misbehavior committed in it, and such fact should be proven, before any of the Judges, that such person or persons, (natives) are or have been harboring such people of the said description and character, he, she or they, (the offenders) shall pay for each and every offense, one hundred dollars, for the benefit of the Cherokee Nation; which amount may be collected by the National Light-horse in any kind of property, to be valued by the Judges before whom the case

---

* Houston had been admitted prior to this date by a special committee appointed John Jolly, but the question of regularity was raised, hence this resolution.

was tried; which property, so valued, and taken, shall be sold by the National Light-horse to the highest bidder, at public auction, on a twelve month's credit, the purchaser to give bond and good security, for the sure payment, drawn payable to the Chiefs of the Cherokee Nation, for the benefit of the Nation.

Tah-lon-tee-skee, December 2, 1833.

Approved—JOHN JOLLY.

———

An Act Prohibiting the Issuing of Due Bills on the National Fund.

Resolved by the National Committee and Council, in General Council Convened, That from and after this date, it shall be unlawful for the National Committee and Council or Chiefs to draw and issue a due bill payable out of the National funds or annuity due bill drawn after this date shall not be valid.

Resolved Further, That from and after this date, all debts, dues or demands, which may become due, against the Cherokee Nation, for services rendered or otherwise created, and the same admitted to be just, and passed by the National Council, shall be registered in the National register by the Clerk of the National Committee, which account, claims, etc., thus admitted and registered, shall be payable out of the National annuity or other National funds.

Tah-lon-tee-skee, December 3, 1833.

Approved—JOHN JOLLY.

———

An Act Prohibiting Negro Slaves to own Property.

Resolved by the National Committee and Council, in General Council Convened, That after the expiration of six months from and after this date, no slave or slaves in the Cherokee Nation, shall have the right or privilege to own any kind of property whatever. And therefore, all slaves in the Cherokee Nation, now owning any kind of property, are hereby required to sell or dispose of it previous to the expiration of said six months. And if any slave or slaves now holding property, and failing to comply with this law, by not selling it off by the above named time, shall thereby forfeit their property to their owners, and the National

Vann House. Erected at Spring Place, Georgia, in the latter part of the Eighteenth Century by James Vann, a half blood Scotch-Cherokee. It was later the residence of his son, Joseph Vann, familiarly known as "Rich Joe" Vann.

Light-horse are hereby required to enforce and carry into effect this law in their respective Districts.

Resolved Further, That if a slave or slaves are caught gambling or intoxicated, or if they should in any way abuse a free person, he, she or they, (negroes) shall for either of the above offenses, receive sixty lashes on the bare back for each and every such offense, to be inflicted by the Light-horse.   H[sic]

Tah-lon-tee-skee, December 3, 1833.

Approved—JOHN JOLLY,
BLACK COAT,
W. WEBBER,
Chiefs.

An Act Relative to Salines.

Resolved by the National Committee and Council, in General Council Convened, That all salines within the limits of the Cherokee Nation are the property of the Cherokee Nation.

Resolved Further, That no person or persons shall have the right to work a saline in the Nation without obtaining a lease for such purpose from the National Council.

Resolved Further, That after the present leases on salines are out, all such salines shall be leased out to the highest bidder, and such bidders shall be entitled to leases on such salines as bid for by giving their bond with approved security. The rents to be paid in cash annually and no lease on a saline shall be given for a longer term than five years at a time.

Resolved Further, That all persons getting leases on salines as above stated, shall furnish their own metal and other preparations necessary for such purpose, (salt kettles, furnace, shed, troughs, sale house and the like are here meant), and when their lease runs out such preparation and the kettles revert to the Nation.

Resolved Further, That where a bond is taken for the rent of a saline, it shall be drawn for double the amount of the annual rent, and made payable to the Chiefs for the benefit of the Nation. And in case any person or persons having such a lease, and if he or they should fail to pay the rent annually such person or persons so failing shall forfeit and pay the Nation the amount of their bond. And in case they should violate the law on salines, or any part of such regulations as are herein

134

mentioned, they shall forfeit their leases and likewise their metals and other preparations mentioned in the foregoing article.

Resolved Further, That no others but citizens of the Nation shall have the right to lease or rent a saline lying within the limits of the Nation, neither shall it be lawful for a citizen of the United States to be taken into partnership, or be sharers in a saline in any way whatever.

Resolved Further, That all the salt now due and which may be due the Nation for the present leases on salines, shall be and is hereby valued at fifty cents per bushel, (50 lbs.,) the sale that is to be issued to individuals excepted, and such persons as now have leases shall have the right to pay the Nation cash at the above rates annually instead of salt.

Tah-lon-tee-skee, December 6, 1833.

Approved—JOHN JOLLY.

An Act Relative to Electing President and Clerks of the National Council.

Resolved by the National Committee and Council, in General Council Convened, That from and after this date, the National Committee and Council shall at the next annual National Council held after their election, as such members, proceed to elect a chairman or president, and a clerk to each House, each House shall act separately and elect its presiding officers, and who shall be elected from among the members of the two Houses respectively, which presiding officers and the clerks shall not be elected for a longer term than the members then in session have to serve, requiring all their terms of services (presiding officers and clerks) to expire at the same time.

Tah-lon-tee-skee, May 8, 1834.

Approved—JOHN JOLLY, Prin'l. Chief.

An Act, Fixing the Pay of Judges and Light-Horse.

Resolved by the Committee and Council, in General Council Convened, That the District Judges shall be allowed for their services, twenty-five dollars each per year, and the National Light-horse, forty dollars each per year, which accounts shall be paid out of the National annuity or other National funds.

135

Tah-lon-tee-skee, May 10, 1834.
Approved—JOHN JOLLY.

An Act Respecting Elections.

Resolved by the Committee and Council, in General Council Convened, That from and after this date, the members of the National Committee and Council, and the officers (Judges and Light-horse) of the Cherokee Nation, shall be elected by a vote of the people, given in at their respective precincts in each District, and for which purpose it is hereby

Further Resolved, That the people of the Cherokee Nation shall meet at their respective precincts in each District once in two years, on the second Monday in July, and proceed to elect by vote, two members of the National Committee and two members of the National Council, which members shall be elected to serve two years from the date of their election; and there shall be also elected at the same time and place two District Judges and two National Light-horse to serve two years from the date of their election, whose duties shall be to serve in their respective Districts as set forth by law.

Resolved Further, That the elections held in each District for the above specific purposes, shall be superintended by the Judges of the same District, and each candidate for the above named offices shall make known to the Judges superintending the elections, which office they design running for; and it shall be the duty of the Judges to have this distinctly understood by the people before voting, after which they can proceed to vote, one at a time by calling the names of such candidates which they judge are the best qualified to fill the office running for, and after all the people present have voted, the Judges shall count out publicly the number of votes given to each one of the candidates took up for the same office, and such candidates as have thereby gained the highest number of votes for the different offices shall thereby be considered duly and lawfully elected to the respective offices for which they were candidates and run for. And it shall be the duty of the Judges as before required under section third to give each member thus elected to the Nation Committee and Council, Judges, and Light-horse, a certificate of their election, which shall be their voucher to the National

Robert Bruce Daniel. Cherokee genealogy No. I—$1^1 1^2 1^3 8^4 1^5$. Assistant Chief of the Cherokee Nation from November, 1871, to January 16, 1872.

Council of such members, Judges and Light-horse having been duly elected according to law.

Resolved Further, That all elections under the law as herein above specified for the purpose of electing members to the National Committee and Council, Judges and Light-horse shall be and are hereby required to be held at the following named places in each District: That is the precinct or place for holding elections under the law; that in Lees Creek District, shall be at the present residence of Little Charles, on Skin Bayou; that in Sallisaw District at Fox's residence on Sallisaw Creek; that in Illinois District at the National Council House (Tah-lon-tee-skee) and that in Neosho District at John Drew's residence on Bayou Menard.

Tah-lon-tee-skee, May 10, 1834.

Approved—JOHN JOLLY, Prin'l. Chief.

An Act Relative to Estate and Administrators.

Resolved by the National Committee and Council, in General Council Convened, That where a citizen of the Cherokee Nation dies, and previous to his death, and while possessed of his natural reason and senses, he or they should make or cause to be made, their written will for the disposition of their property after death, or if they should make verbal, all such wills either written or verbal, and the same attested by two or more good witnesses, shall be valid and binding in law to all intents and purposes, unless the law directs otherwise.

Resolved Further, That if a person should in their will name and appoint a person or persons to administer on the estate, or they should appoint an executor or executors to their will, such person or persons so appointed, shall be the proper and legal administrators of such an estate, or executors of the will thus assigned to them, provided such person or persons so appointed are native of the Cherokee Nation.

Resolved Further, That no will on the estate of a deceased person shall be exempt from the payment and satisfying of all just debts and demands against it, and any such will or other disposition of an estate, and not having in it this provision (payment of all just debts and demands), shall not be valid until it shall have first conformed to this and other regulations of the law.

Further Resolved, That all wills, either written or verbal, on the estates of deceased persons, and also all administrators or executors therein named and appointed as such, shall be inclusively subject to the law regulating estates and wills of deceased persons.

Resolved Further, That all estates of deceased persons after satisfying all just debts and demands against them, the balance of such estates shall be equally divided between the heirs of the deceased, unless otherwise directed by a will of the deceased person, to whom the estate belonged.

Resolved Further, And it is hereby furthermore provided, That where a man and woman are living together as man and wife, and either of them should die without a will, and having no heir or heirs, half of the estate of the deceased, shall belong to the survivor, and the other half to the nearest relatives of the deceased; and if at length, the survivor should die heirless, and without making a will, their estate shall belong to the nearest relatives.

Further Resolved, That all persons, whomsoever, that are, and may be appointed by law, or otherwise chosen to administer on the estates of deceased persons, or as executors to wills shall be, and are hereby required to render in, before the judge of the district, where such an estate, thus in their charge belongs, a just and correct schedule of all the property belonging to the estate they have hereby the charge of, and the judge shall estimate the value thereof, and retain the schedule of the property in his office, and in addition to this, such administrators or executors shall be, and are hereby required to execute a bond in the presence of the judge for double the amount of the estate according to the schedule rendered in, and moreover, to give good security, deemed so by the judge, for their faithful performance and just management of the estate in their charge. And all such bonds shall be drawn payable to the Chiefs of the Cherokee Nation, for the benefit of the heirs of the estate for which the bond was given; which bond and the obligations of the securities attached thereto, shall be retained in the judge's office, until complied with as the law requires, and according to promise.

Further Resolved, That when a person dies without making a will of the property, it shall be, and it is hereby annexed to, and made the duty of the judge of the district where such an estate lies, to appoint one or two suitable persons to administer on and take charge of such an estate, but he shall require such person or persons so appointed in a schedule of all the property belonging to the estate, and to give bond and good security as the law requires.

Further Resolved, That where the estate of a deceased person consists of horses, cattle and hogs, and an executor or administrator is appointed by or according to the law to take charge of such an estate, the administrator or executor, shall be and are hereby allowed for his trouble with the stock, one-third of all the increase of horses and cattle belonging to the estate, and if there be any horses and cattle belonging to the estate, and if there be any hogs they shall be disposed of for the benefit of the heirs of the estate.

Further Resolved, That it is herein provided, That where a person dies, and their estate is in debt, the dwelling houses, and other buildings belonging to the place, and household furniture, the plantation, farming tools and gearing, shall all be exempted from sale, and shall not be used to satisfy debts against the estate, but shall be reserved in all instances whatever, for the use of the survivor and heirs of the estate. All laws to the contrary notwithstanding.

Tah-lon-tee-skee, May 10, 1834.

Approved—JOHN JOLLY.

Thomas Chisholm[*] Elected Third Chief.

Whereas, The Chiefs of the Cherokee Nation have called the National Committee and Council together for the purpose of selecting a Chief to fill the vacancy occasioned by the death of Col. Walter Webber, who occupied the office of Third chief of the Cherokee Nation; now, therefore,

Resolved by the Committee and Council, in General Council Convened, That Thomas Chisholm be, and he is hereby, fully appointed and constituted as such to fill the vacated office of third chief of the Cherokee Nation, who shall serve out the balance of the four-year term the deceased chief had to serve, ending in 1836.

Furthermore, The National Committee and Council have thought it advisable and necessary to have two assistant counselors attached to the Chiefs, and also a clerk, and therefore appoint John Rogers and John Looney to the said station or office, and James Madison Payne, clerk,

---

[*] Thomas Chisholm was he maternal grandfather of United States Senator Robert L. Owen.

which persons are to serve until the present term of the Chiefs is out.
Tah-lon-tee-skee, July 16, 1834.
Approved—JOHN JOLLY, Prin'l. Chief.

An Act Authorizing the Chiefs to Receive Public Moneys.

Resolved by the National Committee and Council, in General Council Convened, That from and after this date, all the annuities which may become due from the United States shall be paid over to the Chiefs, who shall be, and they are hereby authorized to receive and receipt for the same for and in behalf of the Nation, which money shall be kept safely in their hands until the National Council, shall by law, regulate its disposal.
Tah-lon-tee-skee, October 25, 1834.
Approved—JOHN JOLLY.

An Act Relative to Vacancies in the Seats of Absent Members of the National Council.

Resolved by the National Committee and Council, in General Council Convened, That from and after this date, where a member or members of the National Committee or Council is absent, or unable to attend a council, such member's vacancy shall remain void, until the absent member or members are able to take their seats in Council. And such members' vacancies in the National, shall not be filled by other persons as has heretofore been the custom.
Tah-lon-tee-skee, November 4, 1834.
Approved—JOHN JOLLY,
BLACK COAT,
Chiefs.

A Resolution Appointing William Thornton[*] Keeper of Public Records.

Resolved by the National Committee and Council, in General Council Convened, That William Thornton, be, and he is hereby appointed and authorized to take charge of the National papers and documents of the Cherokee Nation, and the clerk of the Chiefs, and the clerks of the National Committee and Council shall be, and are hereby required to render to said person all the public papers and documents (Chiefs' papers excepted) which may be, now or hereafter, in their possession.

Tah-lon-tee-skee, November 4, 1834.

Approved—JOHN JOLLY.

————

Joseph Vann[†] and James Rogers[‡] Elected Second and Third Chiefs.

Thomas Chisholm,[§] Third Chief, having deceased in the autumn of 1834, and Black Coat, Second Chief, having also died in the spring of 1835; the Principal Chief deeming it expedient, has therefore called the National Committee and Council together, and also notified and invited the people generally to attend for the purpose of selecting a Second and Third Chief to fill the vacancies occasioned by the deaths of the two above named Chiefs.

But the people, on account of sickness, being unable to attend generally the National Council has thought it unadvisable to make a permanent selection of the Chiefs at present, it being, however, necessary to have the vacancies filled, the National Council has temporarily appointed Messrs. Joseph Vann and James Rogers to occupy the said vacated offices until the next annual National Council meets, when a regular appointment of Chiefs to the said offices will take place, and preparatory to this arrangement;

Resolved by the National Committee and Council, in General Council Convened, That at the next ensuing National Council, the

————

[*] XVII—$1^1 1^2 1^3$.
[†] Cherokee Genealogy—XVII—$1^1 2^2 2^3$.
[‡] Cherokee Genealogy No. 1—$1^1 1^2 2^3 6^4$.
[§] Cherokee Genealogy—XIII—1^1.

National Committee and Council shall proceed by a joint vote of the two houses to elect a Second and Third chief of the Cherokee Nation, who, when elected, shall serve a term of four years from the date of their election to said offices.

Further Resolved, That the Principal Chief, John Jolly, shall serve out his present term, and at the expiration of which (October, 1836), he shall be reinstated in the same office and the station he now occupies (Principal Chief) for a term of four years more, and the appointment shall be made and performed in a manner according to the former usages and customs of the Cherokees on such occasions.

Tah-lon-tee-skee, June 4, 1835.

Approved—JOHN JOLLY, Prin'l. Chief.

An Act Relative to Public Blacksmith Shops.

Resolved by the National Committee and Council, in General Council Convened, That two persons in each district be and are hereby appointed to superintend the public blacksmith in their respective districts.

Resolved Further, That the two Committee members of each district be, and they are hereby appointed and authorized to superintend the said smiths in their respective districts, whose duty shall be to see that the said smiths do all they are required to do under their instructions from the Agent.   The Committee members of each district to be furnished with a copy of said instructions.

Resolved Further, That in case any of the blacksmiths should fail to do their duty as per orders of the Agent, and the superintendents think it necessary, they can report such smith to the Agents for a further investigation of the case, which smith shall be required to do his duty or remove as the Agent may decide.

Tah-lon-tee-skee, October 26, 1835.

Approved—JOHN JOLLY, Prin'l. Chief.

An Act Relative to the School Funds.

Resolved by the National Committee and Council, in General Council Convened, That the balance of the school fund now due, and which may be due this Nation from the United States Government under

143

the treaty of May 6, 1828, shall be and is hereby equally proportioned between the four districts of this Nation (the balance of division to be governed by former resolution on this fund passed March 27, 1833).

Resolved Further, That each district shall, by and under this resolution have the entire management of their respective portion of said fund to do and act with it as may seem best for promoting and design for which said fund was appropriated.

Resolved Further, That all resolutions passed by the National Council on March 27, 1833, militating against the herein foregoing resolutions, shall, from and after this date, cease to be in force, and are hereby made null and void (the payment at Dr. Palmer's station per resolution of March 27, 1833, not prevented up to this date).

Tah-lon-tee-skee, October 27, 1835.

Approved—JOHN JOLLY, Prin'l. Chief.

Powers and Duties of the Chiefs.

Resolved by the National Committee and Council, in General Council Convened, That the duty of the Chiefs of the Cherokee Nation shall be to sign all acts and resolutions of the National Council, that is, such acts and resolutions as are designed to be laws for the government of the Cherokee people and their Nation.

Resolved Further, That all communications from the National Council to the United States Indian Department, or to an Indian Agent of a general nature and National importance, shall be submitted to the Chiefs for their consideration and approval; likewise, all communications or resolutions of the National Council relating to another Nation or government, and also matters of National importance shall require the approbation and sanction of the Chiefs to make them valid.

Resolved Further, That all treaties or compacts entered into by and between this Nation and another Nation, shall also require the approbation and sanction of the Chiefs, without which such treaties or compacts shall be of no force.

And Resolved Further, That all documents or resolutions of the National Council, partaking of the nature of these herein above mentioned, shall be subject to the Chiefs' consideration, as before specified, and the same shall be submitted to them by the National Council for that purpose, and if the Chiefs refuse to approve of or sanction such documents or resolutions, they shall thereby be null and void, and of no force; but if the Chiefs approve of and sanction them, they shall then be valid, lawful and binding upon the Cherokee Nation.

Resolved Further, That as the executive or head of the Cherokee Government consists of three persons or Chiefs, it shall be, and is therefore hereby required that all three of the Chiefs' signatures shall be affixed or signed to a National document or resolution of the National Council, to cause and make such documents or resolutions valid; that is, such as may be submitted by the National Council for such purpose, and any such document or resolution not having the signatures of all the Chiefs affixed or signed to it, the same shall be void and of no force.

Resolved Further, That it is hereby made the duty of the Chiefs to be present at and attend the annual National Councils if necessary, for the purpose of approving of and sanctioning such documents and resolutions as the National Council may submit to them for that purpose; and it is further hereby understood that not a less number than two of the Chiefs can act officially, and it is therefore required that at least two of them should be together when on duty to cause their acts to be valid.

And it is Furthermore Provided, That in case one of the Chiefs should be unable to attend a National Council or other place, as the case may be, when and where his presence was required, such Chief will have the right to authorize, by giving a certificate to that effect, either of the other two Chiefs to sign his name to any document for him if necessary during his absence, and the same shall be valid and lawful as if the absent Chief had been present and written his own signature.

Further Resolved, That the Chief shall have the right to withhold their approval and sanction to any document or resolution, which may be laid before them by the National Council, if in their opinion, their approval of such document or resolution would be improper or injurious to the welfare of the Cherokee Nation; but it shall be necessary for them to return such document or resolution to the National Council then in session, accompanied with their advice and opinion and also their reasons for withholding their approval and sanction.

Resolved Further, That when a subject is laid before them, (the Chiefs) for their consideration, and they should disagree in opinion, a majority of the same opinion shall rule, that is, if two of the Chiefs are of one opinion, their opinion shall prevail, and equal to a decision and which shall be the same as if all three of them had agreed in opinion, and they can proceed accordingly to approve of and sanction as the case may be.

Resolved Further, That it shall be the duty of the Chiefs to observe the laws of the Cherokee Nation, to look over its welfare and the prosperity of their people, and also to advise the National Council upon matters of National importance, and point out such subjects as they wish the National Council to act upon. But in case any of the Chiefs should so far forget the importance of his station or trust imposed upon him as to violate the duties assigned to him, or do anything contrary to the nature of his office, such Chief shall be tried for the offense committed, by a joint Council, composed of the National Committee and Council of the Cherokee Nation, and the President on the National Committee shall preside over the joint Council for the purpose of sanctioning whatever may be decided upon, but shall not be entitled to a vote while presiding over such a Council.

Resolved Further, That in case any of the Chiefs should be charged with a violation of the duties assigned to him, or of doing anything contrary to the nature of his office, and such Chief or Chiefs, are brought to trial, it shall require a vote of the same opinion, of two-thirds of the said joint Council, to form a decision and confirm an impeachment; and in case in impeachment is confirmed as above specified, such Chief or Chiefs, so impeached, shall thereby forfeit the office as Chief of the Cherokee Nation, and their commission as such, he null and void.

Resolved Further, That all communications of a National Character, to and from this Nation and any other Nation or Government, shall be received by and through the Chiefs. And any public document of the above description transmitted otherwise, shall not be considered official by the National Council.

Resolved Further, That the Chiefs shall have the authority to call a National Council on matters of National importance, if they deem it expedient, and necessary, but on common matter, they can act themselves, and it is furthermore provided, that the Chiefs can send expresses on public business at the Nation's expense, but shall be required to give their expenses in a certificate to the National Council specifying the length of time the expresses were on duty.

Tah-lon-tee-skee, October 29, 1835.

Approved—JOHN JOLLY, Prin'l. Chief.

146

David Rowe. Cherokee genealogy No. II—$1^1 4^2 4^3 12^4$.
Assistant Chief of the Cherokee Nation from November,
1875, to November, 1879.

EARLY HISTORY OF CHEROKEES.

Resolution Relative to Filling the Vacancies of the Office of Chiefs.

Resolved by the National Committee and Council, in General Council Convened, That whenever a vacancy occurs in the first or second Chiefs' stations before their term is out, caused by death or by resignation, or by removal from office of either of the said Chiefs, the next Chief or Chiefs in rotation, as the case may be, shall be promoted to fill the vacancies thus occasioned, or if a vacancy should occur in the Second Chief's station by promotion, the same regulation shall be observed, so that in all instances, where a vacancy occurs in the first or second Chief's station, the vacancy may finally fall on the Third Chief's station, in order that the Chief to be elected to fill the vacancy shall come in as Third Chief; and it shall not be lawful under any circumstances whatever, for a new Chief to be elected to a station, ahead of the senior Chiefs in office before their term is out; and where a vacancy occurs in the Third Chief's station, by the death of the Third Chief, or by any of the foregoing circumstances, before such Chief's term is out, the vacancy shall be filled by electing, as the law directs, another Chief, to that station, but he shall not be elected for a longer term than to serve out the balance of the term the vacated Chief had to serve at the time that his station became vacant. And, also, in no instance shall a Chief's term for which he was first elected, be prolonged or shortened, on account of his being promoted—in order that all the Chiefs (three in number) terms may expire at the same time.

Tah-lon-tee-skee, October 29, 1835.
Approved—JOHN JOLLY, Prin'l. Chief.
JOSEPH VANN, Second Chief.
JAMES ROGERS, Third Chief.

An Act Prohibiting Citizens of the United States From Keeping Public Tables.

Resolved by the National Committee and Council, in General Council Convened, That from and after this date, none other than citizens of the Cherokee Nation shall keep a tavern or public table at a Council or public gathering in the Cherokee Nation (fruit, flour and bacon not prohibited from being brought in for sale), and any person or persons not citizens of the Nation, violating this law shall forfeit and pay the Nation one hundred dollars, to be collected forwith, by the National Light-horse.

Tah-lon-tee-skee, November 14, 1835.

Approved—JOHN JOLLY, Prin'l. Chief.

JOSEPH VANN, Second Chief.

JAMES ROGERS, Third Chief.

TEXAS CHEROKEES.

The principal man among the Texas Cherokees was Richard Fields,[*] an eighth-blood Cherokee. His maternal great grandparents were Grant, a Scotchman, and a full-blood Cherokee woman;[†] his grandparents were William Emory and—Grant,[‡] the former an Englishman and the latter a half-blood Cherokee; his parents were Richard and Susannah Fields nee Emory; his father was an American and his mother a quarter-blood Cherokee.

He was a half brother of Bushyhead, the father of Chief Justice Jesse Bushyhead and of John Martin, who was the first Chief Justice and first Treasurer of the Cherokee Nation.[§]

Fields was a man of considerable intelligence, and although he spoke the English language fluently and preferably, he was not able to sign his name. While a delegate to the City of Mexico in 1822-23 he was made a Master Mason.

The first mention of land cession in Texas, as far as I am able to find, is in a letter from Fields to James Dill, alcalde of Nacogdoches. The letter correct is as follows:

February 1st, 1822.

Application made to the Supreme Governor of the Province of Spain.

Dear Sir:—I wish to fall at your feet and humbly ask you, what must be done with us poor Indians? We have some grants that were

---

[*] $I-1^1 1^2 3^3 2^4$.

[†] $I-1^1$.

[‡] $I-1^1 1^2$.

[§] Starr's Cherokee Genealogy $I-1^1 1^2 3^3 9^4$.

given to us when we lived under Spanish government and we wish you to send us news by the next mail whether they will be reversed or not. And if we were permitted, we will come as soon as possible to present ourselves before you in a manner agreeable to out talents.

If we do present ourselves in a rough manner, we pray you to right us. Our intentions are good toward the government.

Yours as a Chief of the Cherokee Nation,

RICHARD FIELDS.[‖]

This letter in the original, was much garbled, and from the peculiar phraseology and marked servility of tone, I suspect that it was written by the free negro, William Goings, who lived in that section and was often interpreter for the Indians.

No further record of the Cherokees are shown until on the following November, when the following agreement was entered into at Bexar"

"Articles of an agreement, made and entered into between Captain Richard, of the Cherokee Nation, and the Governor of the Province of Texas.

"Article 1st. That the said Chief Richard, with five others of his tribe, accompaniled[sic] by Mr. Antonio Mexia and Antonio Wolfe, who act as interpreters, may proceed to Mexico,,[sic] to treat with his Imperial Majesty, relative to the settlement which said Chief wishes to make for those of his tribe who are already in the territory of Texas, and also for those who are still in the United States.

"Art. 2nd. That the other Indians in the city, and who do not accompany the before mentioned, will return to their village in the vicinity of Nacogdoches, and communicate to those who are at said village, the terms of this agreement.

"Art. 3rd. That a party of the warriors of said village must be constantly kept on the road leading from the province to the United States, to prevent stolen animals from being carried thither, and to apprehend and punish those evil disposed foreigners, who form assemblages, and abound on the banks of the River Sabine within the territory of Texas.

[‖] Bexar Archives.

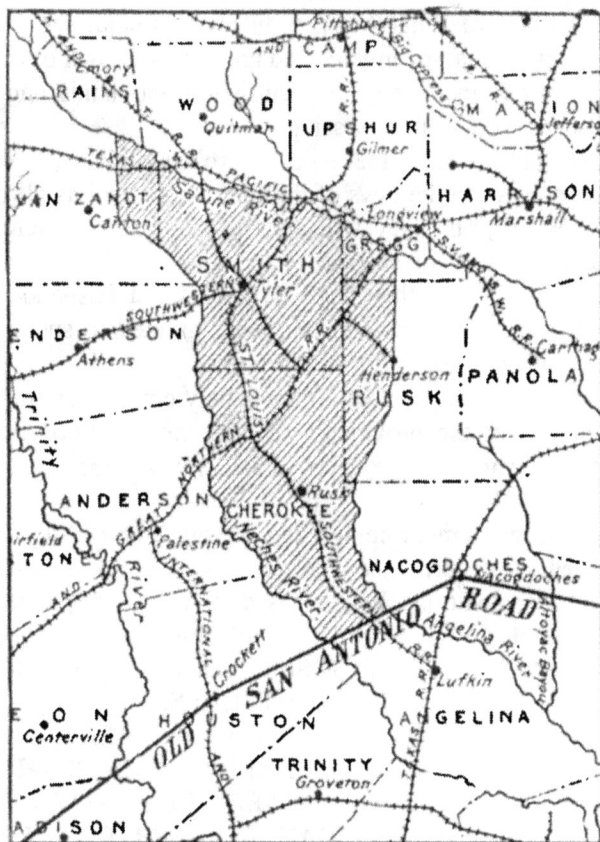

Map of the Cherokee Land Grant in Texas.

"Art. 4th. That the Indians who return to their town, will appoint as their chief the Indian captain call Kunetand, alias Tong Turqui, to whom a copy of this agreement will be given, for the satisfaction of those of his tribe, and in order that they may fulfill its stipulations.

"Art. 5th. That meanwhile and until the approval of the Supreme Government is obtained, they may cultivate their lands and sow their crops, in free and peaceful possession.

"Art. 6th. That the said Cherokee Indians, will become immediately subject to the laws of the Empire, as well as all others who may tread her soil, and they will also take up arms in defense of the nation, if called upon to do so.

"Art. 7th. That they shall be considered Hispano-Americans, and entitled to all the rights and privileges granted to such; and to the same protection, should it become necessary.

"Art. 8th. That they can immediately commence trade with the other inhabitants of the province, and with the exception of arms and ammunitions of war, with the tribes of savages who may not be friendly to us.

"Which agreement comprising the eight preceding articles, has been executed in the presence of twenty-two Cherokee Indians, of the Baron de Bastrop, who has been pleased to act as interpreter, of two of the Ayuntamiento, and two officers of this Garrison. Bexar, 8th November, 1822.   JOSE FELIX TRESPALACIOS,
JOSE FLORES,
NABOR VILLARREAL,
RICHARD FIELDS—X—His Mark,
EL BARON DE BASTROP,
MANUEL ITURRI CASTILLO,
FRANCO DE CASTANEDO."[*]

On the same day that this agreement was made, Governor Trespalacios wrote the following note to Don Gaspar Lopez, commandant general of the Eastern Internal Provinces, transmitting it by Lt. Don Ignacio Ronquillo:

"Captain Richard (Fields) of the Cherokee Nation, with twenty-two more Indians that accompanied him, visited me to ask permission for

---

[*] Record of Translations of Empresario Contracts, 85; Texas General Land Office.

all belonging to his tribe to settle upon the lands of this province. After I had informed myself through foreigners, who are acquainted with this Nation, that it is the most industrious and useful of the tribes in the United States, I entered with said Captain into an agreement, the original of which I send you. This arrangement provided that Captain Richard and six others of his Nation, with two interpreters, escorted by Lt. Don Ignacio Douquillo[sic] and fifteen men of the Viscayan, shall proceed to your headquarters and, if it meet your approval, thence to the court of the Empire.

"The Cherokee Nation, according to their statement, numbers 15,000 souls; but there are within the borders of Texas only one hundred warriors and two hundred women and children. They work for their living, and dress in cotton cloth, which they themselves manufacture. They rise cattle and horses and use firearms. Many of them understand the English language. In my opinion they ought to be useful to the province, for they immediately became subjects to its laws, and I believe will succeed in in putting a stop to carrying stolen animals to the United States, and in arresting those evil-doers that infest the roads."[*]

Fields arrived in Mexico City in the spring of 1823, and commenced negotiations with the authorities of the empire for recognition of the rights of the Cherokees in the province of Texas, but to add to other embarrassments, Emperor Iturbide was forced to abdicate, on March 19th, 1823; and on the 30th of the same month the supreme executive power was vested in Victoria, Bravo and Negrete.

The revolutionary spirit of the time created chaotic conditions under which legislative action was erratic and the tendency became generally subversive to the actions of the previous regime.

On April 27th, 1823, Lucas Alaman, Minister of Relations, addressed the following communication to Felipe de la Garza, who had succeeded Lopez as Commandant General of the Eastern Internal Provinces:

"The Supreme Executive Power has been pleased to resolve, that Richard Fields, chief of the Cherokee Tribe of Indians, and his companions, now in this Capital, may return to their country, and that they be supplied with whatever may be necessary for that purpose. Therefore, Their Supreme Highnesses have directed me to inform you,

[*] Bexar Archives.

that although the agreement made on 8th November, 1822, between Richard Fields and Colonel Felix Trespalacios, Governor of Texas, remains provisionally in force, you are nevertheless, required to be very careful and vigilant, in regard to their settlements, endeavoring to bring them towards the frontier, and at places least dangerous, not permitting for the entrance of any new families of the Cherokee tribe, until the publication of the General Colonization Laws, which will establish rules and regulations to be observed, although the benefits to arise from it can not be extended to them, in relation to all of which, Their Highnesses intend to consult the sovereign Congress. That while this is effecting, the families already settled, should be well treated, and the other chiefs also, treated with suitable consideration, provided that those already within our territory respect our laws, and are submissive to our authorities; and finally, Their Highnesses order, that in the future neither these Indians, nor any others be permitted to come to the City of Mexico, but only send their petitions in ample form, for journeys similar to the present, are of no benefit, and only create unnecessary expense to the State.

"All of which I communicate to you for your information and fulfillment."

Shortly after the issuance of the resolution of April 27th, 1823, Fields and his associates returned home, where he claimed that the Mexican government had granted the Indians whom he represented "territory sufficient for me and that part of the tribe of Indians dependent on me to settle on." This land was described by Antonio Wolfe (whose name was variously spelled by the Spaniards as "Gulfo," "Bulfo" ad "Bulfe"), the interpreter who accompanied Fields to Mexico City, as "lying between the Trinity and Sabine rivers north of the San Antonia road."[*]

On March 6th, 1824, Fields wrote as follows to the Governor at San Antonio: "It was my intention on my return from Mexico to present myself at San Antonio in order that the authorities there might examine the papers which I received from the superior government of the nation. But it was impossible to do this, because a party of Comanches had prepared an ambush on the road. However, I had the good fortune to escape them.

"The superior government has granted me in this province a

---

[*] Bexar Archives.

territory sufficient for me and that part of the tribe of Indians dependent on me to settle on, and also a commission to command all the Indian tribes and nations that are in the four eastern provinces.

"I pray your honor to notify all the Indians within your territory, and particularly the Lipans, that on the 4th of July next, I shall, in compliance with the order of the supreme government, hold a general council of all the Indian tribes, at my house in the rancheria of the Cherokees, twelve miles west of the Sabine river. At this council I shall propose a treaty of peace to all Indians who are willing to subject themselves to the orders of the government. In case there should be any who may not wish to ratify what I propose, I shall use force of arms to subdue them.

"I beg you to notify the commandant at San Antonio that he shall, for the satisfaction of his people, send some trusted person to aid in the treaty of peace and see how the affair is managed.

"Should it be convenient, have this letter translated, and have the authorities send it to Rio Grande and Monclova, in which two places I left copies of the documents from the superior government."[†]

The intertribal council, which was later changed to August 20th, met at Fields' residence, embraced all the tribes in Texas, except the Comanches and Tonkawas, on whom Fields proposed to wage war.[*]

On April 15th, 1825, the authorities of the State of Texas, notwithstanding that the State Colonization law provided for granting lands to such Indians as the Cherokees,[‡] granted to Benjamin Edwards a right to settle eight hundred families on land occupied by the Cherokees since 1820.

Edwards issued a notice on October 25th, "that whatsoever families or persons residing within the bounds of said territory, and all those who pretend to hold claims to any parts of the land or lands of said territory shall immediately present themselves and exhibit their titles and documents, if they have any, in order that they may be approved or rejected, according to law; and if they do not do this, said lands shall be sold without further question."

[†] Bexar Archives.
[*] Bexar Archives.
[‡] Article 19, of the General Colonization Law of Mexico, of August 18, 1824.

The diplomatic duplicity of the Mexican government was such that much unrest was prevalent among not only the Cherokees, but also among the American settlers in the eastern portion of Texas; land tenure was insecure, and life and property in constant jeopardy.

A large number of Indians from the United States joined the Texas Cherokees in 1826, and an able representative was dispatched by Fields to the City of Mexico, in the person of John Dunn Hunter, to look after the rights of his people; in doing this Fields was following the time-honored custom of the Cherokees in the United States in sending delegations to the seat of the central government.

As a last resort a compact was entered into between the Cherokees and the Edwards brothers, to safeguard their mutual rights. This compact was as follows:

"Whereas, The Government of the Mexican United States, have, by repeated insults, treachery, and oppression, reduced the White and Red emigrants from the United States of North America, now living in the Province of Texas, within the territory of said government, which they have been deluded by promises solemnly made, and most basely broken, to the dreadful alternative of either submitting their freeborn necks to the yoke of an imbecile, unfaithful, and despotic government, miscalled a Republic; or of taking up arms in defense of their inalienable rights and asserting their independence; they—viz: The white emigrants now assembled in the town of Nacogdoches, around the Independent Standard, on the one part, and the red emigrants who have espoused the same Holy Cause, on the other, in order to prosecute more speedily and effectually the war of Independence, they have mutually undertaken, to a successful issue, and to bind themselves by the ligaments of reciprocal interests and obligations, have resolved to form a treaty of Union, League and Confederation.

"For the illustrious object, Benjamen W. Edwards and Harmon B. Mayo, agents of the Committee of Independence, and Richard Fields and John D. Hunter, the agents of the red people, being respectfully furnished with due powers, have agreed to the following articles:

"1. The above named contracting parties, bind themselves to a solemn Union, League, and Confederation, in peace and war, to establish and defend their mutual independence of the Mexican United States.

2. The contracting parties guaranty, mutually, to the extent of

their power, the integrity of their respective Territories, as now agreed upon and described, viz: The Territory apportioned to the Red people, shall begin at the Sandy Spring, where Bradley's road takes off from the road leading from Nacogdoches to the Plantation of Joseph Dust, from thence West, by the Compass, without regard to variation, to the Rio Grande, thence to the head of the Rio Grande, thence with the mountains to the head of the Big Red River, thence north to the boundary of the United States of North America, thence with the same line to the mouth of Sulphur Fork, thence in a right line to the beginning.

The territory apportioned to the White People, shall comprehend all the residue of the Province of Texas, and of such other portions of the Mexican United States, as the contracting parties, by their mutual efforts and resources, may render independent, provided the same shall not extend further west than the Rio Grande.

3. The contracting parties mutually guaranty the rights of Empresarios to their premium lands only, and the rights of all other individuals, acquired under the Mexican Government, and relating or appertaining to the above described territories, provided the said Empresarios and individuals do not forfeit the same by an opposition to the independence of the said Territories, or by withdrawing their aid and support to its accomplishment.

4. It is distinctly understood by the contracting parties, that the Territory apportioned to the Red people, is intended as well for the benefit of those tribes now settled in the Territory apportioned to the White people, as for those living in the former Territory, and that it is incumbent upon the contracting parties for the Red people to offer the said tribes a participation in the same.

5. It is also mutually agreed by the contracting parties, that every individual, Red or White, who has made improvements within either of the Respective Allied Territories and lives upon the same, shall have a fee simple of a section of land including his improvement, as well as the protection of the government in which he may reside.

6. The contracting parties mutually agree, that all roads, navigable streams, and all other channels of conveyance within each Territory, shall be open and free to the use of the inhabitants of the other.

7. The contracting parties mutually stipulate that they will direct all their sources to the prosecution of the Heaven-inspired cause which has given birth to this solemn Union, League and Confederation, firmly

relying upon their united efforts, and the strong arm of Heaven, for success.

In faith whereof the Agents of the respective contracting parties hereunto affix their names. Done in the Town of Nacogdoches, this, the twenty-first day of December, in the year of our Lord, one thousand eight hundred and twenty-six.

RICHARD FIELDS,	B. W. EDWARDS,
JOHN D. HUNTER.	H. B. MAYO,

"We, the Committee of Independence, and the Committee of the Red people, do ratify the above Treaty, and do pledge ourselves to maintain it in good faith. Done on the day and date above mentioned.

RICHARD FIELDS,	MARTIN PARMER, President.
JOHN D. HUNTER,	HAYDEN EDWARDS,
NE-KO-LAKE,	W. B. LEGON,
JOHN BAGS,	JNO. SPROWL,
CUK-TO-KEH.	B. J. THOMPSON,
	JOS. A HUBER,
	B. W. EDWARDS,
	H. B. MAYO.

At the conclusion of this compact, Hunter and Fields returned immediately to the Cherokee settlement, and urged compliance with the stipulations of the agreement, but in the meantime Peter Ellis Bean and other Mexican emissaries had by alluring promises of land and personal preferment been able to detach many Cherokees from the alliance. The Kickapoos, one of the allied tribes, refused to co-operate with the Fredonians on account of their extreme enmity to the Whites.

At the same time Samuel[sic] F. Austin and other friends of the Mexican government exerted themselves in spreading disaffection among even the Fredonians.

Such were the influences brought to bear that by January 1, 1827, less than twenty Cherokees could be brought to Nacogdoches by Hunter and Fields, and the force of the Fredonians was not any larger.

Austin, Bean and others used every effort to break Hunter and Fields from what now, even to them, seemed a hopeless cause, but their honor and the sense of justice of their cause would not allow them to desert it.

Bowl, who had become a Mexican sympathizer, had Hunter and Fields killed in 1827, while they were in the Cherokee settlement attempting to raise further reinforcements; Bowl secured the papers of Fields, and turned over at least a portion of them to the Mexican authorities.

Thus at the instigation of the authorities, the two most intelligent Indian advocates were decimated, and the papers on which they based their claims, confiscated.

On March 11, 1827, Mateo Ahumada, commander of the Department of Texas, wrote his superior officer, Anastasio Bustamante, Commandant of the Eastern Internal States, as follows: "Justice obliges me to inform you that Mush and Bowls—civil and military chiefs of the Cherokees—agreed to and gave orders to kill Hunter and Fields, recovering the papers and flag mentioned, and giving me every proof of loyalty to and love for our government, from which they hope for a grant of some land in the district for settlement of their tribe, which solicitation I commend to your Excellency very particularly. I beg that you will take it into consideration in order that the reward may be granted them which they have earned by the valuable services they have rendered, and in view of the fact that they have offered to arrest and to deliver Edwards and other leaders of that faction in case they should cross to this side of Sabine river and visit their village."[*]

Bustamante's reply to this on April 7 was: "With your communication of March 11, last, I received without delay the documents and revolutionary flag mentioned. It is with pleasure that I learn of the complete restoration of public tranquility in that district.

The death of those perfidious demagogues, Fields and Hunter, is certainly a very fortunate circumstance for the happiness of the tribes, who were led astray, and for the preservation of the integrity and peace of that territory which they claimed to rule. On which account I have particularly recommended to the Supreme Government the merits of Mush and Bowls, who commanded a breach of the pledge with said visionaries and offered to arrest for you the Edwardses and as many of the rebels as recrossed the Sabine to stir up the tribes.

Likewise I have recommended the application of these chiefs with regard to the granting of the lands which they solicit for the regular settlement of their tribe, which no doubt will be done by the Supreme Government; and I hope that you will induce them to settle where they

---

[*] Bexar Archives.

may be happy and contribute permanently and in a profitable manner toward the pacification of the Comanches. Aided by our troops and fellow citizens of Bexar, it seems to me that the land most productive and best suited to the attainment of both objects is the San Saba canon; but, if they should insist that lands be granted them on the frontier, let it be where it best suits the interests of the Mexican Republic, consulting, as far as possible, the good of the Cherokees, to whose present chiefs you will offer the assurances of my special esteem, and give me due notice of what they finally say relative to the selection of lands in order that I may report it to his excellency, the President of the Republic."[*]

In July, 1827, Bowl was given a commission as lieutenant-colonel by the Mexican Government. With this and other personal favors and adulations, the vanity of Bowl and other leaders among the Cherokees was gratified, and they made few requests of the Government.

General Teran, who, in April, 1830, had succeeded General Bustamante, wrote, on August 15, 1831, to Governor Letona, that he had asked the Cherokees to select the land that they wished; which they did select on the Trinity and Sabine rivers, and he requested that a commissioner be appointed to place the Cherokees in possession of their land and give the titles to the same.[†]

Col. Jose de las Piedras was commissioned, on March 22, 1832, by Governor Letona, to vest the Cherokees with titles to their lands.[‡]

Col. Piedras asked additional instructions in regard to his duties, and this was complied with, but before he received them, he had been expelled by an uprising at Nacogdoches, on August 2, 1832.

In rapid succession the other two officers on whose action the destinies of the Cherokees depended, died; Governor Letona died of yellow fever and General Teran committed suicide; the latter was succeeded in January, 1833, by Vincente Filisola, and through this appointment the Cherokees were placed in a disadvantageous position, as Filisola himself was a grantee of lands embracing the Cherokee lands.

---

[*] Bexar Archives.
[†] Record of Translations of Empresario Contracts, 89.
[‡] Yoakum's History of Texas, page 299.

David McNair Faulkner.   Cherokee genealogy No. XV—
$1^1 1^2 2^3 5^4 2^5$.   Assistant Chief of the Cherokee Nation from
November, 1903, until June 30, 1914.

On July 20, 1833, the Cherokees submitted to the Political Chief the following petition: "The subscribers have been appointed commissioners by the Cherokee tribe of Indians to solicit from the government of the State of Coahuila and Texas a title to a certain tract of land which said government offered to them for the establishment of a colony of their tribe.

The subscribers state that the tract they have selected under the promise of the Government is located in the vicinity of Nacogdoches, and is bounded as follows: Boundary begins where the Bexar road crosses the Trinity river, and follows said road in the direction of Nacogdoches to the Angelina river; thence it proceeds up the right bank of said Sabine river to its headwaters; thence west till it touches the Trinity river; and finally from thence down the left bank of said Trinity river to the point of beginning.

The subscribers represent to you that, after the Government had promised to give them said tract, they settled in it, and from that time forward have cultivated it in hope of securing complete ownership. But some years having passed since the Government made them that promise, they request that the Government send a commissioner to put them in possession, for which office they recommend Don Manuel Santos Coy, a resident of Nacogdoches and qualified to carry out this commission.

The subscribers state further that some Americans have selected for their own use the best places within the tract pointed out, and that they stated to the chiefs of the tribe that these acts were authorized by the Government.* The subscribers have been duly appointed by the members of said tribe to arrange this matter, to request of the Government the favor of putting them in possession of said tract of land immediately, and to ask that the commissioner be instructed to grant a title for the whole tract, to be held in community.

In addition, it is absolutely necessary that the Americans be removed, who settled on said tract after the subscribers had a claim to it by virtue of a promise made them by the Government, or, at least, that the land which they have selected be not taken from that belonging to

---

* Most of these settlers had been located under the grants of David G. Burnet and General Filisola. These grants were made several years subsequent to the Cherokee settlement on the lands in question.

this tribe.

    The subscribers further state that it is now four years since they sent to the Government the census of the population of their tribe, and that since that time there has been an increase in the number of individuals of the tribe amounting to one hundred and ninety or two hundred persons. This increase is due to our boys growing into men and to the immigration of our fathers and brothers, who have come to live with us. We desire that these persons be entitled to the same privileges as those who came earlier, comprising about two hundred men, and the total number of persons being about eight hundred. The property of this tribe consists of about three thousand head of cattle, about the same number of hogs, and five or six hundred head of horses. The subscribers inform you that said tribe lives chiefly by tilling the soil and raising cattle. They believe that the lands designated will be sufficient for their farms and ranches.[†]

COL. BOLES,[‡]

JOHN BOLES,[§]

RICHARD JUSTICE,

PIGGEON,[‖]

ANDREW VANN,[¶]

ELI HARLIN.[**]

    In the summer of 1833, Andrew M. Vann, Col. Bowl and Eli Harlin, Cherokee delegates, visited Monclova, capital of the province of Cohuila[sic] and Texas, and their rights were further recognized by the following document: "Citizen Jaun Martin de Beramendi, vice-governor of the Free State of Coahuila and Texas, exercising the supreme executive power:

    "Colonel Boles, Andrew M. Vann and Eli Harlin of the Cherokee Nation, having presented themselves before me in this capital for the purpose of obtaining proprietorship of the tract of land which the

---

[†] Record of Translations of Empresario Contracts; General Land Office of Texas; 85 and 86.

[‡] Starr's Cherokee Genealogy—VII—1^1.

[§] Starr's Cherokee Genealogy—VII—1^11^2.

[‖] Starr's Cherokee Genealogy—XXI—1^12^2.

[¶] Starr's Cherokee Genealogy—II—$1^14^24^34^4$.

[**] Starr's Cherokee Genealogy—III—$111^28^31^4$.

said Nation at present occupies in the department of Bexar, I caused an examination to be made of the points in the report, which the political chief of that department enclosed in his letter of July 20th, last, and which the representatives named above have delivered. It being noticed that said Indians have located their habitations on the headwaters of the Angelina and of the Cherokees,* which points are included in the colonization grants of the foreigner David G. Burnet[sic] and of General Don Vincente Filisola, it is not possible to grant the aforesaid petition; because the time allowed to said empresarios for completing their contracts has not yet expired.

In reply to this objection, the petitioners stated that for nine years they have lived in that part of the State under my charge by permission of the supreme general government, granted to said Boles and Richard Fields in the City of Mexico; and that they believe themselves in possession of better rights than the said empresarios, because their grant is older. Notwithstanding, they have no other documentary evidence than the word which the supreme chief of the Republic gave them, and a map that he delivered to them, on which was designated the territory, the same now occupied by them.

In consideration of all the above, I have directed that said tribe shall not be disturbed for any reason whatever, until the supreme general government may decide whether in truth it granted to said tribe the concession to which reference has been made at the aforementioned time, or until the termination of the extension of time that the honorable Congress has granted to David G. Burnett. In either case the chief of said tribe shall be notified, so that by means of an attorney he may be represented in this capital for the purpose of concluding a suitable contract.

For the security and protection of the Cherokee tribe, which henceforth subjects itself to the constituted authorities of the state under my charge, I give these presents in the city of Monclova, on the twenty-first day of August, in the year one thousand eight hundred and thirty-three.

BERAMENDI."†

---

* The words "and of the Cherokees: is most probably an error of either the translator or the printer.

† Appendix to Empressario Contracts, 111,300.

DeWitt Clinton Lipe. Cherokee genealogy No. VI—$1^1 1^2 2^3 1^4 7^5 2^6$. Treasurer of the Cherokee Nation from 1879 to 1883, and first County Clerk of Rogers County, Oklahoma.

By this it will be seen that the Cherokees were again delayed in the specific possession of deeds to their lands until the contracts of Filisola and Burnett had expired. The dates of these expirations were December 21, 1835.[‡]

But again the grim nemesis of fate interposed, and on November 11th, of that year, the Consultation of Texas, adopted the "plan of Provisional Government," and by that means extinguished Mexican authority in Texas.

In its struggle for existence the incipient Republic of Texas found itself in dire straits; twenty or thirty thousand people were defending themselves against eight millions[sic].

Thousands of Indians were within her borders, and if they allied themselves with the Mexicans the chances of the Texans would thereby be rendered more precarious. Among these, the Cherokees wielded a dominant influence, and measures were taken on the second day of the inchoate government to attach as firmly as possible this civilized tribe which, with its allies, was at that time a formidable force.

To attain this object, the legislative body of the Republic, which was denomniated[sic] the "consultation," passed the following decree:

"Be It Solemnly Decreed, That we, the chosen delegates of the Consultation of all Texas, in general convention assembled, solemnly declare that the Cherokee Indians, and their associate bands, twelve tribes in number, agreeably to their last general council in Texas, have derived their just claims to lands, included within the bounds hereinafter mentioned from the Government of Mexico, from whom we have also derived our rights to the soil by grant and occupancy.

"We solemnly declare that the boundaries of the claims of the said Indians, to land, is as follows, to-wit: Lying north of the San Antonio road, and the Neches, and west of the Angelina and Sabine rivers. We solemnly declare that the governor and General Council, immediately on its organization shall appoint commissioners to treat with the said Indians, to establish the definite boundary of their territory and secure their confidence and friendship.

"We solemnly declare that we will guarantee to them the peaceful enjoyment of their rights to their lands, as we do our own; we solemnly declare, that all grants, surveys and location of lands, within the

[‡] Decree 192, Laws of Coahuila and Texas.

bounds hereinbefore mentioned, made after the settlement of said Indians, are, and of right, ought to be utterly null and void, and that the commissioners issuing the same, be and are hereby ordered, immediately to recall and cancel the same, as having been made upon lands already appropriated by the Mexican Government.

"We solemnly declare that it is our sincere desire that the Cherokee Indians, and their associate bands, should remain our friends in peace and war, and if they do so we pledge the public faith for the support of the foregoing declarations.

"We solemnly declare that they are entitled to our commisseration[sic] and protection, as the just owners of the soil, as an unfortunate race of people that we wish to hold as friends, and treat with justice. Deeply and solemnly impressed with these sentiments as a mark of sincerity your committee would respectfully recommend the adoption of the following resolution

"Resolved, That the members of this convention, now present, sign this declaration, and pledge the public faith, on the part of the people of Texas.

"Done in convention at San Felipe de Austin, this 13th day of November, A. D., 1835.

(Signed)   B. T. ARCHER, President.

John A. Wharton, Meriwether W. Smith, Sam Houston, William Menifee, Chas. Wilson, Wm. N. Sigler, James Hodges, Wm. W. Arrington, John Bevil, Wm. S. Fisher, Alex. Thompson, J. G. V. Pierson, D. C. Barrett, R. Jones, Jesse Burnam, Lorenzo de Zavala, A. Horton, Edwin Waller, Daniel Parker, Wm. P. Harris, John S. D. Byrom, Wm. Whitaker, A. G. Perry, Albert G. Kellogg, C. C. Dyer, Geo. M. Patrick, J. D. Clements, Claiborne West, Jas. W. Parker, J. S. Lester, Geo. w. Davis, Joseph L. Hood, A. E. C. Johnson, Asa Hoxey, Martin Parmer, Asa Mitchell, L. H. Everett, R. M. Counterman Williamson, Philip Coe, R. R. Royal, John W. Moore, Benj. Fuga, Sam T. Allen, Wyatt Hanks, James W. Robinson, Henry Millard, Jesse Grimes, A. B. Hardin, Wyly Martin, Henry Smith, David B. Macomb, A. Houston, E. Collard.

P. B. DEXTER, Secretary."

To further cement this community of interests, the "General Council of the Provisional Government of Texas" passed, on December 26th, the following resolution:

"That Sam Houston, John Forbes and John Cameron be, and they are hereby appointed, commissioners to treat with the Cherokee Indians and their twelve associate bands, under such instructions as may be given them by the Governor and Council, and should it happen that all the commissioners cannot attend, any two of them shall have power to conclude a treaty and report the same to the General Council of the Provisional Government for its approval and ratification."[*]

Four days later the General Council, in conference with the above given resolution, instructed the commissioners, as follows:

"Be It Resolved, etc., by the General Council of the Provisional Government of Texas:

"Section 1. That Sam Houston, John Forbes and John Cameron, appointed commissioners to treat with the aforesaid Indians, be, and they are hereby instructed to proceed as soon as practicable to Nacogdoches and hold a treaty with the Indians aforesaid, and that they shall in no wise transcend the declarations made by the Consultation on November last in any of their articles by treaty.

"Sec. 2. That they are required in all things to pursue a course of justice and equity towards the Indians and protect all honest claims of the white, agreeably to such laws, compacts or treaties, as the said Indians may heretofore have made, with the Republic of Mexico, and that the said commissioners be instructed to provide in said treaty with the Indians that they shall never alienate their hands, either separately of collectively, except to the Government of Texas, and to agree that the said Government will, at any time hereafter, purchase all their claims at a fair and reasonable valuation.

"Sec. 3. That the Governor be required to give the commissioners such definite and particular instructions as he may think necessary to carry into effect the foregoing resolutions, together with such additional instructions as will secure the effective co-operation of the Indians at a time when it may be necessary to call the effective force of Texas into the field and agreeing for their services, in a body, for a specified time.

"Sec. 4. That the commissioners be authorized and empowered to exchange other lands within the limits of Texas, not otherwise appropriated, in place of the lands claimed by said Indians and their

[*] Passed December 22, 1835.

associate bands."[†]

The object of the proposed negotiations is clearly shown as to "secure the effective co-operation of the Indians at a time when it may be necessary to call the effective force of Texas into the field." The action of the General Council in conciliating the Cherokees and their allied tribes at this time would appeal to any one as a wise course to pursue; but what of the wisdom, if policy alone should be the dictator, of the Cherokees, in espousing the cause of the Texans, whose straggling bands were generally numbered by units and tens, illy clad, variously armed, and without artillery or commissariat, and opposed by the regular arm of an organized general government, whose troops were, in all reports and rumors of the day, mentioned in numbers of hundreds and thousands, adequately financed, and commanded by Santa Ana, and heralded "Napoleon of the West."

On February 4th, 1836, Santa Ana left Monclova with a well equipped army, that was variously given at six thousand[‡] veterans, his triumphal March for two months is evidenced by all historians, and in one instance, where the commander's escutcheon might have been graven by honorable victory, his perfidious butchery instead, rendered the name Alamo a synonym of massacre.

Samuel Houston, commander-in-general of the army of the Republic of Texas, with his few hundred men, which was one of the bravest fighting forces that ever graced American soil, daily retreated in front of his formidable opponent, amid a clamor of censure from a people, few of whom had ever head[sic] of Fabius.

On February 23rd, the same day that Santa Ana invested the Alamo, Samuel Houston and John Forbes, "commissioners on the part of the Provisional Government of Texas," concluded the following treaty with Colonel Bowl, Big Mush and others, representatives of the Cherokees and their associate bands, whereby peace and commercial relations were established, the Cherokee boundaries defined and their land guaranteed to them.

[†] Passed December 26, 1835, and approved December 28, 1835.
[‡] Letter from President Santa Anna, Annual Report of the American Historical Association, Vol. 11, page 96.

A TREATY BETWEEN TEXAS AND THE TEXAS CHEROKEES.

This treaty made and established between Sam Houston and John Forbes, Commissioners on the part of the Provisional Government of Texas, on the one part, and the Cherokees and their associate bands now residing in Texas, of the other part, to-wit: Shawnees, Delawares, Kickapoos, Quapaws, Choctaws, Boluxies, Jawanies, Alabamas, Cochaties, Caddos of the Naches, Tahovcattakes and Unatuquous, by the Head Chiefs, Head Men and Warriors of the Cherokees, as elder Brother and Representative of all the other Bands, agreeable to their last General Council. This treaty is made conformably to a declaration made by the last General Consultation, at St. Felipe, and dated 13th November, A. D. 1835.

Article First.

The parties declare that there shall be a firm and lasting peace forever, and that a friendly intercourse shall be preserved by the people belonging to both parties.

Article Second.

It is agreed and declared that the before named Tribes or Bands shall form one community and that they shall have and possess the lands within the following bounds, to-wit: lying West of the San Antonio road and beginning on the West at the point where the said road crosses the river Angelina, and running up said river, until it reaches the mouth of the first large creek—below the Great Shawnee Village—emptying into the said river from the Northeast, thence running with said creek to its main source, and from thence, a due north line to the Sabine River, and with said river west, then starting where the San Antonio road crosses the Angelina river and with the said road to the point where it crosses the Naches river and thence running up the East side of said river, in a northwest direction.

Article Third.

All lands granted or settled in good faith previous to the settlement of the Cherokees, within the before described bounds, are not conveyed by this treaty, but excepted from its operation. All persons who have once been removed, and returned, shall be considered as

170

intruders and their settlements not be respected.

Article Fourth.

It is agreed by the parties aforesaid, that the several Bands or Tribes, named in this treaty, shall all remove within the limits or bounds as before described.

Article Fifth.

It is agreed and declared by the parties aforesaid, that the land lying and being within the aforesaid limits, shall never be sold or alieniated[sic] to any person or persons, power or Government whatsoever else than the Government of Texas, and the Commissioners on behalf of the Government of Texas, bind themselves, to prevent in future all persons, from intruding within the said bounds. And it is agreed on the part of the Cherokees for themselves and their younger Brothers, that no other tribes or bands of Indians whatsoever shall settle within the limits aforesaid, but those already named in this treaty and now residing in Texas.

Article Sixth.

It is declared that no individual person, member of the Tribes before named, shall have power to sell or lease land to any person or persons, not a member or members of this Community of Indians, nor shall any citizen of Texas be allowed to lease or buy land from any Indian or Indians.

Article Seventh.

That the Indians shall be governed by their own regulations and laws, within their own territory, not contrary to the laws of the Government of Texas. All property stolen from the citizens of Texas, or from the Indians shall be restored to the party from whom it was stolen, and the offender or offenders shall be punished by the party to whom he or they may belong.

Article Eighth.

The Government of Texas shall have power to regulate trade and intercourse, but no tax shall be laid on the trade of the Indians.

Article Ninth.

The parties to this treaty agree that one or more agencies shall be created and at least one agent shall reside specially within the Cherokee Village, whose duty it shall be to see that no injustice is done to them, or other members of the community of Indians.

Article Tenth.

The parties to this treaty agree, that as soon as Jack Steele and Samuel Benge shall abandon their improvements without the limits of the before recited tract of country and remove within the same—that they shall be valued and paid for by the Government of Texas—the said Jack Steele and Samuel Benge, having until the month of November, next succeeding from the date of this treaty, allowed them to remove within the limits before described. And that all the lands and improvements now occupied by any of the before named bands or tribes not lying within the limits before described, shall belong to the Government of Texas and subject to its disposal.

Article Eleventh.

The parties of this treaty agree, and stipulate that all the Bands or Tribes, as before recited (except Steele and Benge) shall remove within the before described limits within eight months from the date of this treaty.

Article Twelfth.

The parties to this treaty agree that nothing herein contained shall effect the relations of the Sabine or the Naches, nor the settlers in the neighborhood thereof, until a General Council of the several bands shall take place and the pleasure of the convention of Texas be known.

Article Thirteenth.

It is also declared, That all the titles issued to lands not agreeably to the declaration of the general consultation of the people of all Texas, dated the thirteenth day of November, eighteen hundred and thirty-five, within the before recited limits—are declared void—as well as all orders and surveys made in relation to the same.

Done at Colonel Bowl's Village on the twenty-third day of

February, eighteen hundred and thirty-six, and the first year of the Provisional Government of Texas.

Signed:	Sam. Houston,
	John Forbes,
Witness,	*his*
his	Colonel x Bowl
Fox x Fields,	*mark*
mark	*his*
	Big x Mush,
Henry Millard,	*mark*
	his
	Samuel x Benge,
Joseph Durst,	*mark*
	his
A. Horton,	Oozovta x
	mark
	his
George W. Case,	Corn x Tassell,
	mark
	his
Mathias A. Bingham,	The x Egg,
	mark
George V. Hockley,	John Bowl,
	his
Sec'y of Commission.	Tunnetee x
	mark

DEPARTMENT OF STATE

Austin, Texas, Dec. 7th, 1870.

I, **James P. Newcomb**, Secretary of State of the State of Texas, hereby certify that the above and foregoing is a

> Seal of the
> Department
> of the
> State of
> Texas.

true and correct copy of the original on file in this office, in testimony whereof, I have hereunto signed my name and caused the Seal of the Department of State to be affixed, day and date as above written.

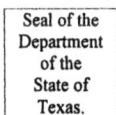

Signed:

JAMES P. NEWCOMB,

Per J. E. OLDRIGHT,   Secretary of State.

Acting Sec'y of State.

This negotiation through General Houston hastened to join his hard-pressed and needy command. For some two months more, in order to save his valiant little army, he voluntarily suffered the censure and condemnation of the ignorant, intriguing and vicious; but the glorious day of retribution was at hand, for on April 21st, 1836, Houston with seven hundred and fifty men, attacked and annihilated Santa Ana's command of sixteen hundred at San Jacinto, the President became a prisoner of war in the camp of Houston, and Texas was free.

The Republic of Texas, an established government, was soon officially recognized by the civilized nations of the earth, and her southern boundary lines had been defined by a treaty with Mexico. Settlers from the north and east had swelled the population to such an extent that Texas had no further reason to fear her only enemy, and former suzerain. She was a free moral agent bound only by her self-imposed constitutional limitations; and with accredited power, dreamed new dreams, conjured up new thoughts, and days of distress were forgotten; the rights of the Cherokee settlers was disputed and pretexts for their expulsion was sought.

On December 10th, 1838, Mirabeau B. Lamar was inaugurated third president of the Republic of Texas; and in his inaugural address he said in relation to the Cherokee claims that "The sword shall mark the boundaries of the Republic." David G. Burnett, who claimed a Mexican land grant, made in the early thirties, covering a considerable portion of the Cherokee concessions, was elected vice-president.

In July, 1839, Indian Agent Lacy, Dr. W. G. W. Jowers and John H. Reagan, then a young man, twenty years of age, visited the Cherokees on the Angelina with propositions for their disposal of their homes, these commissioners being in a short time, joined by Vice and Acting President David G. Burnett, Secretary of War Albert Sidney Johnston and Adjutant General Hugh McLeod. Three regiments of Texas soldiery accompanied the treaty delegation to within a few miles of the Cherokee settlement, where they pitched their camps.

Caleb L. and Jennie Starr. Cherokee genealogy No. III—$1^1 1^2 4^3 8^4 5^5 6^6$ and $1^1 1^2 4^3 8^4 5^5 7^6$, younger brother and sister of the author.

The Cherokees were loth[sic] to leave the homes that they had occupied since 1820; they argued that they were the earliest settlers in this vicinity, and that they had been peaceable and law abiding; their consent to deportation could not be gained; the negotiators on the part of the Republic returned to the military camp and reported the futility of their efforts.

The immediate subsequent events were given by Hon. John H. Reagan in the following language:

"An agreement was made that neither party was to break up camp or make any move without giving notice to the other party. On the 13th or 14th of July, Colonel Burleson's regiment of regulars, and Colonel Landrum's regiment of volunteers, reached the camp of the Texas forces. And early in the morning of the 15th Chief Bowles sent his son, John Bowles, accompanied by Fox Fields, under a flag of truce, to notify the Texans that he would break up camp that morning and move to the west of the Neches river. On reaching headquarters under a flag of truce, they delivered their message to General Johnston, and having done so, inquired if they could return in safety. They both spoke English very well. General Johnston told the messenger that his father had acted honorably in giving notice according to agreement, and that he would see that they had safe conduct out of our camp; and he detailed a number of men, with orders to see them safely a half mile beyond our line of pickets. He also told them to inform Chief Bowles that the Texas forces would break up camp that morning and pursue him.

On the assembling of this little army of three regiments, the volunteers wanted General Rusk for their commander, while the regulars preferred Colonel Burleson for that position. These two patriots and heroes of the Revolution, which made Texas a Republic, did not desire to antagonize each other, and either of them was willing that the other should command. But it was agreed to solve the question by having General Kelsey H. Douglas elected as brigadier general and placed in chief command. And when this army broke up its camp on the morning of the 15th of July, 1839, to pursue the Indians, Colonel Landrum was ordered to move up on the east side of the Neches river, and be in position to intercept the Indians if they should turn northward, as it was expected they would. The regiments of Colonel Rusk and Colonel Burleson moved to the west, passing though the camp which had been occupied by the Indians, and crossing the Neches on their trail.

"Chief Bowles had taken position on a creek some six miles west of the Neches with a part of his warriors, and had sent the familes[sic] with the balance of the warriors, to a position six miles north of where he made his stand. His men occupied the bed of a creek, which, running from north to south, made a sudden bend to the east, and his position was immediately above this bend.

After the Texans crossed the Neches, scouts were thrown forward, with directions if they found the Indians in position to give battle, to keep up a desultory firing at long range, without exposing themselves too much, so as to give notice of the position of the Indians. As the command advanced, and when the firing of the scouts was heard, Colonel Rusk's regiment was ordered to advance on the north side of the creek they were on, and Col. Burleson's regiment was ordered to cross the creek and advance on the south side of the creek, so as to put the Indians between these regiments. When the troops reached the bend of the creek, which was the extreme right of the line occupied by the Indian, Rusk's regiment wheeled to the right and formed in front of the Indians, while Burleson's regiment turned to the right and passed up in the rear of the Indians. This was an hour or two before sundown. A battle ensued, which, however, did not last long. Dr. Rogers and Colonel Crain were killed and some six or eight Texans were wounded; and it was reported that the Indians left eighteen dead on the field, and the remainder of them were routed and joined the others some six miles to the north, near the Neches, and just north of the Delaware village. The Texans camped for the night near the battlefield. And fearing that the Indians might break up into small bands and attack the more exposed frontier settlements, a number of squads were detached from the command and ordered to proceed to the exposed parts of the frontier to defend the families of the whites.

On the morning of the 16th of July, the Texans, thus reduced in number, took up the line of march in pursuit of the Indians, and found them, soon after passing the Delaware village, in a very strong position. They occupied a long ravine, deep enough to protect them, with gently sloping open woods in from of them. Our line of battle was formed on a low ridge in front of them, and skirmishers thrown forward, who were at once engaged with the skirmish line of the Indians. Every sixth man of our command was detailed to hold and guard our horses. This, with the details sent away the night before, had considerably reduced our fighting force, and we were confronted by the entire force of the Indians, which, from the information we afterwards received, considerably outnumbered the Texans who participated in the battle.

"The scene at that time made a very vivid impression on my young mind. The Delaware village, in our immediate rear, was wrapped in flames, and the black columns of smoke were floating over us; the skirmishers were fighting in front of us, and our line of battle advancing to the conflict.

"The battle lasted about two hours. We had six men killed and thirty-six wounded. The Indian loss was very much greater. During this engagement Chief Bowles was a very conspicuous figure. He was mounted on what we call a paint horse, and had on him a sword and sash and military hat and silk vest, which had been given him by General Houston. And thus conspicuously mounted and dressed, he rode up and down the rear of his line, very much exposed during the entire battle. Our officers two or three times ordered the men to advance nearer the line of the Indians, and then would order them to fall back, in hope that in this way the Indians might be drawn from their strong position. And just as this was done the last time word run along our line that the Indians were in our rear getting our horses. This came near producing a panic. Col. Len Williams and Ben A. Vansickle, who were with us, and who understood and could speak the Cherokee language, told us that at that time they could hear Bowles, who was urging his warriors to charge, and telling them that the whites were whipped if they would charge.

"When at last the Indians retreated, Chief Bowles was the last one to attempt to leave the battlefield. His horse had been wounded many times and he was shot through the thigh. His horse was disabled and could go no further, and he dismounted and started to walk off. He was shot in the back by Henry Conner, afterwards Major Conner; walked forward a little and fell, and then rose in a sitting position, facing us, and immediately in front of the company to which I belonged. I had witnessed his dignity and manliness in council, his devotion to his tribe in sustaining their decision for war against his judgment, an[sic] his courage in battle, and wishing to save his life, ran toward him, and, as I approached him from one direction, my captain, Robert Smith, approached him from another, with his pistol drawn. As I got to him, I said, 'Captain, don't shoot him,' but as I spoke he fired, shooting the Chief in the head."

Clement Vann Rogers. Cherokee genealogy No. II—
$1^1 4^2 4^2 11^4 2^5$.   Captain in the Confederate Cherokee
service, Cherokee Senator and a member of the Oklahoma
State Constitutional Convention.

"* * * After the battle, our command camped at the edge of the bottom very near the Indians, but made no attack on them. That night we could hear the hum and bustle of their camp the greater part of the night, and the next morning they were gone in the direction of the Grand Saline, in what is now Van Zandt county; and while our troops followed them to the Grand Saline, they did not overtake them."[*] Colonel Bowl, was, by his own statement, eighty-three years of age at the time of his death.[†]

The "Texas Cherokees" returned to, and became citizens of the Cherokee Nation, Indian Terrotory[sic].

Through all their vicissitudes Houston remained the friend of the Cherokees.

Colonel Bowl was a halfblood Cherokee; his mother was a fullblood and his father—from whom he inherited auburn hair and a very fair complexion—was a Scotchman.

LIGHTHORSE.

Resolved by the Chiefs and Warriors in a National Council assembled, That it shall be, and is hereby authorized, for the regulating parties to be organized to consist of six men in each company; one Captain, one Lieutenant and four privates, to continue in service for the term of one year, whose duties it shall be to suppress horse stealing and robbery of other property within their respective bounds, who shall be paid out of the National annuity, at the rates of fifty dollars to each Captain, forty to the Lieutenant, and thirty dollars to each of the privates; and to give their protection to children as heirs to their father's property, and to the widow's share whom he may have had children by or cohabited with, as his wife, at the time of his decease, and in case a father shall leave or will any property to a child at the time of his decease, which he may have had by another woman, then, his present wife shall be entitled to receive any such property as may be left by him or them, when substantiated by two or one disinterested witness.

Be it resolved by the Council aforesaid, When any person or

---

[*] "Expulsion of the Cherokees from East Texas," John H. Reagan, page 43.
[†] Ibid, page 41.

persons which may or shall be charged with stealing a horse, and upon conviction by one or two witnesses, he, she, or they, shall be punished with one hundred stripes on the bare back, and the punishment to be in proportion for stealing property of less value; and should the accused person or persons raise up with arms in his or their hands, as guns, axes, spears and knives, in opposition to the regulating company, or should they kill him or them, the blood of him or them shall not be required of any the persons belonging to the regulators from the clan the person so killed belonged to.

Accepted—BLACK FOX, Principal Chief.
CHAS. HICKS, Sec'y to Council.
Brooms Town, 11th Sept. 1808.

ABROGATION OF CLAN CUSTOMS.

Be it known, That this day, the various clans or tribes which compose the Cherokee Nation, have unanimously passed by an act of oblivion for all lives for which they may have been indebted, one to the other, and have mutually agreed that after this evening the aforesaid act shall become binding upon every clan or tribe; and the aforesaid clans or tribes, have also agreed that if, in future, any life should be lost without malice intended, the innocent aggressor shall not be accounted guilty.

Be it known, also, That should it happen that a brother, forgetting his natural affection, should raise his hand in anger and kill his brother, he shall be accounted guilty of murder and suffer accordingly, and if a man has a horse stolen, and overtakes the thief, and should his anger be so great as to cause him to kill him, let his blood remain on his own conscience, but no satisfaction shall be demanded for his life from his relatives or the clan he may belong to.

By order of the seven clans.
TURTLE AT HOME,
Speaker of Council,
Approved.— BLACK FOX, Principal Chief,
PATH KILLER, Sec.d
TOOCHALER.
CHAS. HICKS, Sec'y to the Council.
Oostanallah, April 10, 1810.

CONSTITUTIONAL ACT.

Whereas, fifty-four towns and villages have convened in order to deliberate and consider on the situation, of our Nation, in the disposition of our common property of lands, without the unanimous consent of the members of Council, and in order to obviate the evil consequences resulting in such course, we have unanimously adopted the following form for the future government of our Nation:

Art. 1st. It is unanimously agreed that there shall be thirteen members elected as a Standing Committee for the term of two years, at the end of which term they shall be either re-elected or others; and in consequence of the death or resignation of any of said Committee, our head Chiefs shall elect another to fill the vacancy.

Art. 2nd. The affairs of the Cherokee Nation shall be committed to the care of the Standing Committee; but the acts of this body shall not be binding on the Nation in our common property and without the unanimous consent of the members and Chiefs of the Council, which they shall present for their acceptance of dissent.

Art. 3d. The authority and claim of our common property shall cease with the person or persons who shall think proper to remove themselves without the limits of the Cherokee Nation.

Art. 4th. The improvements and labors of our people by the mother's side shall be inviolate during the time of their occupancy.

Art. 5th. This Committee shall settle with the Agency for our annual stipend, and report their proceedings to the members and Chiefs in Council; but the friendly communications between our head Chiefs and the Agency shall remain free and open.

Art. 6th. The above articles for our government, may be amended at our electional term, and the Committee is hereby required to be governed by the above articles, and the Chiefs and Warriors in Council, unanimously pledge themselves to observe strictly the contents of the above articles.

Whereunto we have set our hands and seals at Amoah, this 6th day of May, one thousand eight hundred and seventeen.

Approved in Council, on the day and date above written.

EHNAUTAUNAUEH,
Speaker of the Council.

Approved of the within government by the head Chief,
PATH KILLER.
A McCOY, Sec'y to the Council.
CHAS. HICKS.

USEFUL INDIVIDUALS ACT.

Unanimously agreed, That schoolmasters, blacksmiths, millers, saltpeter and gunpowder manufacturers, ferrymen and turnpike keepers, and mechanics, are hereby privileged to reside in the Cherokee Nation under the following conditions, viz:

Their employers procuring a permit from the National Committee and Council for them and becoming responsible for their good conduct and behavior, and subject to removal for misdemeanor; and further agree, that blacksmiths, millers, ferrymen and turnpike keepers, are privileged to improve and cultivate twelve acres of ground for the support of themselves and families, should they please to do so.

JNO. ROSS, Pres't Nat'l Com.
A. McCOY, Cl'k Nat'l Com.
In Committee, New Town, Oct. 26th, 1819.
In Committee, New Town, Cherokee Nation,
October 30th, 1819.

AN ACT RELATING TO TURNPIKES.

Whereas, The Big Rattling Gourd, Wm. Grimit, Betsy Broom, the Dark, Daniel Griffin, and Mrs. Lesley, having lodged complaint before the Chiefs, of a certain company of persons having formed a combination, and establishing a turnpike arbitrarily, in opposition to the interest of the above named persons, proprietors of a privileged turnpike on the same road:

Be it now, therefore known, That said complaint having been submitted by the Council to the National Committee for a decision, and after maturely investigating into the case, have decreed, that the said new company of the disputed turnpike shall be abolished, and that the above persons are the only legal proprietors and privileged company to establish a turnpike on the road leading from widow Fool's, at the forks

183

of Hightower and Oostenallar[sic] river to Wills creek, by way of Turkey Town; and the said company shall be bound to keep in repair said road, to commence from the first creek east of John Fields, Sr., known by the name, where Vann was shot, and to continue westward to the extent of their limits, and that the widow Fool shall also keep in repair, for the benefit of her ferry at the fork, the road to commence from the creek above named to where Ridge's road now intersects said road east of her ferry, and that the Ridges shall also keep in repair the road to commence at the Two Runs, east of his ferry, and to continue by way of his ferry as far as where his road now intersects the old road, leading from the fork west of his ferry; and that also the Hightower turnpike company shall keep in repair the road from the Two Runs to where it intersects the Federal road, near Blackburn's; and

Be it hereby resolved, That no person or persons whatsoever, shall be permitted to cut out any road or roads leading from any main road now in existence, so as to intersect the same again and to the injury of the interest of any person or persons residing on said road, without first getting an order from the National Council for the opening of said road; and person or persons violating this decree, contained in the foregoing resolution, shall be subject to such punishment and fine as the National Council and Committee may hereafter decide and inflict, on such case as may be brought before them for trial.

JNO. ROSS, Pres't Com.

his

Approved—PATH x KILLER,

mark

CHAS. HICKS.

A. McCOY, Clerk.

New Town, Cherokee Nation, November 2nd, 1819.

INTER-MARRIAGE LAW.

Resolved by the National Committee and Council, That any white man who shall hereafter take a Cherokee woman to wife be required to marry her legally by a minister of the gospel or other authorized person, after procuring license from the National Clerk for that purpose, before he shall be entitled and admitted to the privilege of citizenship, and in order to avoid imposition on the part of any white man.

184

Resolved, That any white man who shall marry a Cherokee woman, the property of the woman so married, shall not be subject to the disposal of her husband, contrary to her consent, and any white man so married and parting from his wife without just provocation, shall forfeit and pay to his wife such sum or sums, as may be adjudged to her by the National Committee and Council for said breach of marriage, and be deprived of citizenship, and it is also resolved, that it shall not be lawful for any white man to have more than one wife, and it is also recommended that all others should also have but one wife hereafter. By order of the National Committee.

JNO. ROSS, Pres't N. Com.

his
Approved— PATH x KILLER,
mark
CHAS R. HICKS.

New Town, Cherokee Nation, October 20th, 1820.

EIGHT DISTRICTS AUTHORIZED.

Resolved by the National Committee and Council, That the Cherokee Nation shall be laid off into eight districts, and that a council house shall be established in each district for the purpose of holding councils to administer justice in all causes and complaints that may be brought forward for trial, and one circuit judge, to have jurisdiction over two districts, to associate with the district judges in determining all causes agreeable to the National laws, and the marshals to execute the decisions of the judges in their respective districts, and the District Councils to be held in the spring and fall seasons, and one company of light horse to accompany each circuit judge on his official duties, in his respective districts, and to execute such punishment on thieves as the Judges and Council shall decide, agreeably to law, and it shall be the duty of the marshals to collect all debts, and shall be entitled to eight per cent, for the same; and the Nation to defray the expenses of each District Council, and in case of opposition to the marshals in execution of their duty, they shall be justifiable in protecting their persons from injury in the same manner as is provided for the National light horse by law.

By order of the National Committee.

JNO. ROSS, Pres't N. Com.

185

his
Approved— PATH x KILLER,
mark
CHAS R. HICKS.
A. McCOY, Clerk.

EIGHT DISTRICTS CREATED.

Resolved by the National Committee and Council, That the Cherokee Nation be organized and laid off in Districts, and to be bounded as follows:

1st. The first District shall be called by the name of Chickamauga, and be bounded as follows: beginning at the mouth of Aumuchee creek, on Oostennallah river, thence north in a straight course to a spring branch between the Island and Rackoon village, thence a straight course over the Lookout Mountain, where the heads of Will's and Lookout creeks oppose against each other on the Blue Ridge, thence a straight course to the main source of Rackoon creek, and down the same into the Tennessee river, and up said river to the mouth of Ooletiwah[sic] creek, and up said creek to take the most southeastern fork, thence a southern course to the mouth of Sugar creek, into the Cannasawgee[sic] river, and down the said river to its confluence with Oostennallah river, and down the same to the place of beginning.

2d. The second District shall be called by the name of Chattooga, and be bound as follows: beginning on the mouth of Rackoon creek, in the Tennessee river, and down the said river to the boundary line, commonly called Coffee's line, and along said line where it strikes Will's creek, and down the said creek to its confluence with the Coosa river, and thence embracing the boundary line between the Cherokee and Creeks, run by Wm. McIntosh and other Cherokee Commissioners by their respective Nations, running southeastwardly to its intersection with Chinubee's trace, and along said trace leading eastwardly by Avery Vann's place, including his plantation, and thence on said trace to where it crosses the Etowah river, at the old ford above the fork, and down said river to its confluence with Oostannallah river, and up said river to the mouth of Aumuchee creek, and to be bounded by the first District.

3d. The third District shall be called by the name of Coosawatee, and bounded as follows: beginning at the widow Fool's ferry, on Oostannallah river, where the Alabama road crosses it, along said wagon road eastwardly, heading towards Etowah town to a large creek above Thomas Pettit's plantation, near to the Sixes, and said creek, northeastward, to its source; thence a straight course to the head of Talloney creek, up which the Federal road leads, thence a straight course to the Red Bank creek, near Cartikee village, thence a straight course to the head source of Potato Mine creek, thence a straight course to the head of Clapboard creek, thence a straight course to the most southern head source of Cannasawgee river, thence a northwestern course to Cannasawgee river, to strike opposite to the mouth of Sugar creek, into the Cannasawgee river and to be bounded by the first and second Districts.

4th. The fourth District shall be called by the name of Amoah, and be bounded as follows: beginning at the head source of Cannasawgee river, where the third District strikes the said source, thence eastwardly a straight course to Spring Town, above Hiwassee Old Town, thence to the boundary line run by Col. Houston, where it crosses Sloan creek, thence westwardly along said line to the Hiwassee river, thence down said river into the Tennessee river, and down the same to the mouth of Ooliatiwah creek, and to be bounded by the first and third Districts.

5th. The fifth District shall be called by the name of Hickory Log, and shall be bounded as follows: beginning at the head of Potatoe[sic] Mine creek, on the Blue Ridge, thence southeastwardly along the Blue Ridge to where Cheewostoyeh path crosses said ridge, and along said path to the head branch of Frog Town creek, and down the same to its confluence with Tahsantee, thence down Chestotee river, thence down the same into the Chattahoochee river, and down the same to the shallow wagon ford on said river, above the standing Peach Tree, thence westward along said wagon road leading to —— Town to where it crosses Little River, a fork of the Etowah river, and down the same to its confluence with Etowah river, and down the same in a direct course to a large creek, and up said creek to where the road crosses it to the opposite side, to be bounded by the Third district.

William Penn Adair. Cherokee genealogy No. XV—$1^11^22^32^41^5$. Colonel in the Confederate Cherokee service and Assistant Chief of the Cherokee Nation from November, 1879, to October 21, 1880.

6th. The sixth District shall be called by the name of Etowah, and be bounded as follows: beginning on the Chattahoochee river, at the shallow wagon ford on said river, and down the same to the Buzzard Roost, where the Creek and Cherokee boundary line intersects the said river, thence along said boundary line westward, to where it intersects Chinubee's trace, and to be bounded by the fifth and third Districts, leaving Thomas Pettit's family in Etowah District.

7th. The seventh District shall be called by the name of Tahquohee, and be bounded as follows: beginning where Col. Houston's boundary line crosses Slare's creek, thence along said boundary line southeastwardly to the Unicoy turnpike road, and along said road to where it crosses the Hiwasee[sic] river, in the Valley Towns, thence a straight course to head source of Coosa creek, on the Blue Ridge above Cheewostoyeh and along said Ridge eastwardly, where the Unicoy turnpike road crosses it and thence a direct course to the head source of Persimmon creek, thence down the same to the confluence of Tahsantee, and with the Frog Town creek, and to be bounded by the third, the fourth and fifth Districts.

8th. The eighth District shall be called by the name of Aquohee, and be bounded as follows: beginning where the seventh District intersects the Blue Ridge, where the Unicoy turnpike road crosses the same, thence eastwardly along said Ridge to the Standing Man, to Col. Houston's boundary line, thence along said line to the confluence of Nauteyalee, and Little Tennessee river, thence down the same to Tallassee village, thence along said boundary line westwardly, to where it intersects the Unicoy turnpike road, and to be bounded by the seventh District; and that each District shall hold their respective Councils or Courts, on the following days:

The first Mondays in May and September for Chickamauga District; and on the

First Mondays in May and September for Coosawatee District; and the

Second Monday in May and September for Amoah District; and on the

First Mondays in May and September for Hickory Log District; and on the

Second Mondays in May and September for Etowah District; and on the

First Mondays in May and September for Aquohee District; and on the

Second Mondays in May and September for Tahquohee District; and each of the Councils or Courts shall sit five days for the transaction of business at each term.

By order of the Committee and Council.

CHAS. R. HICKS.

New Town, Cherokee Nation, November 2d, 1820.

NATIONAL COUNCIL APPORTIONED.

Resolved by the National Committee and Council, That each District shall be entitled to four members to represent them in the National Council, and that each member shall be allowed one dollar per day for their services during the sitting of the Councils, and that a Speaker to the Council be appointed and allowed one dollar and fifty cents per day for his services, and the clerk of the Council be allowed two dollars and fifty cents per day, and that the two principal Chiefs, viz: The Path Killer, shall be allowed one hundred and fifty dollars per annum, and Charles R. Hicks two hundred dollars per annum, considering the burden of writing and interpreting which devolves on him entitles him to this difference; and

Be it resolved, also, That each Committeeman be allowed two dollars per day and the President of the Committee be allowed three dollars and fifty cents a day, and their clerk two dollars and fifty cents per day during the sitting of the National Council, and a member of the Committee shall be chosen as an Interpreter and be allowed fifty cents per day in addition to his pay.

By order of the National Committee.

JNO. ROSS, Pres't N. Com.

EHNAUTAUNAUEH,

Speaker of Council.

his

Approved—PATH x KILLER,

mark

CHAS. HICKS.

A. McCOY, Clerk.

New Town, Cherokee Nation, November 8th, 1822.

190

PROHIBITORY ACT.

Whereas, the great variety of vices emanating from dissipation, particularly from intoxication and gaming at cards, which are so prevalent at all public places, the National Committee and Council, seeking the true interest and happiness of their people, have maturely taken this growing evil into their serious consideration, and being fully convinced that no nation of people can prosper and flourish or become magnanimous in character, the basis of whose laws are not founded upon virtue and justice; therefore, to suppress, as much as possible, those demoralizing habits which were introduced by foreign agency.

Resolved by the National Committee, That any person or persons, whatsoever, who shall bring ardent spirits within three miles of the General Council House, or to any of the courthouses within the several Districts during the General Council, or the sitting of the courts, and dispose of the same so as to intoxicate any person or persons whatsoever, the person or persons so offending shall forfeit his or their whiskey, the same to be destroyed; and be it further

Resolved, That gaming at cards is hereby strictly forbidden, and that any person or persons whomsoever, who shall game at cards in the Cherokee Nation, such person or persons so offending shall forfeit and pay a fine of twenty-five dollars, and further, any person or persons whatsoever, who may or shall be found playing cards at any house or camp, or in the woods within three miles of the General Council House, or any of the courthouses of the several Districts, during the session of the General Council, or sitting of the District Courts, such person or persons so offending shall forfeit and pay a fine of fifty dollars each for every such offense, and that any person or persons, whatsoever, who shall bring into the Cherokee Nation and dispose of playing cards, such person or persons, being convicted before any of the Judges, Marshals or light horse, shall pay a fine to twenty-five dollars for every pack of cards so sold, and it shall be the duty of the several Judges, Marshals and light horse companies to take cognizance of such offenses and to enforce the above resolution.

And be it further resolved, That all fines collected from persons

191

violating the above resolution, the money so collected shall be paid into the National treasury. To take effect and be in full force from and after the first day of January next.

By order of the National Committee.

JNO. ROSS, Pres't N. Com.

his

Approved—PATH x KILLER,

mark

A. McCOY, Clerk of Com.

ELIJAH HICKS, Clerk of Council.

New Town, Cherokee Nation, November 11th, 1824.

MISCEGINATION[sic] ACT.

Resolved by the National Committee and Council, That intermarriages between negro slaves and Indians or whites shall not be lawful, and any person or persons permitting and approbating his, her or their negro slaves to intermarry with Indians or whites, he, she or they, so offending, shall pay a fine of fifty dollars, one-half for the benefit of the Cherokee Nation; and

Be it further resolved, That any male Indian or white man marrying a negro woman slave, he or they shall be punished with fifty-nine stripes on the bare back, and any Indian or white woman marrying a negro man slave shall be punished with twenty-five stripes on her or their bare back.   By order of the National Committee.

JNO. ROSS, Pres't N. Com.

his

Approved—PATH x KILLER,

mark

A. McCOY, Clerk of Com.

ELIJAH HICKS, Clerk of Council.

Miss Clara Melton. Cherokee Genealogy No. III—$1^13^22^36^42^52^61^72^8$.
Graduated from the Cherokee National Female Seminary on May 27, 1909.

BILL OF RIGHTS.

For the better security of the common property of the Cherokee Nation, and for the protection of the rights and privileges of the Cherokee people, we, the undersigned members of the Committee and Council, in legislative Council convened, have established, and by these presents do hereby declare the following articles as a fixed and irrevocable principle, by which the Cherokee Nation shall be governed. These articles may be amended or modified by a concurrence of two-thirds of the members of the Committee and Council in legislative council convened; viz:

Art. 1st. The lands within the sovereign limits of the Cherokee Nation, as defined by treaties, are, and shall be, the common property of the nation. The improvements made thereon and in the possession of the citizens of the Nation, are the exclusive and indefeasible property of the citizens respectively who made, or may rightfully be in possession of them.

Art. 2d. The annuities arising from treaties with the United States, and the revenue arising out of the tax laws, shall be founded in the National Treasury, and be the public property of the Nation.

Art. 3d. The legislative Council of the Nation shall alone possess the legal power to manage and dispose of, in any manner by law, the public property of the Nation, provided, nothing shall be construed in this article so as to extend that right and power to dispossess or divest the citizens of the Nation of their just right to the houses, farms and other improvements in their possession.

Art. 4th. The Principal Chiefs of the Nation shall in no wise hold any treaties, or dispose of public property in any manner without the express authority of the legislative Council in session.

Art. 5th. The members of the Committee and Council, during the recess of the legislative Council, shall possess no authority or power to convene Councils in their respective districts, or to act officially in any matters of concern to the public affairs of the Nation, excepting expressly authorized or delegated by the legislative Council in session.

Art. 6th. The citizens of the Nation, possessing exclusive and indefeasible right to their respective improvements, as expressed in the first article, shall possess no right or power to dispose of their improvements to citizens of the United States, under such penalties as

194

may be prescribed by law in such cases.

Art. 7th. The several courts of justice in the Nation shall have no cognizance of any case transpiring previous to the organization of courts by law, and which case may have been acted upon by the chiefs in council, under the then existing custom and usage of the Nation, excepting there may be an express law embracing the case.

Art. 8th. The two Principal Chiefs of the Nation shall not, jointly or separately, have the power of arresting the judgments of either of the courts or of the legal acts of the National Committee and Council, but that the judiciary of the Nation shall be independent and their decisions final and conclusive; Provided, always, That they act in conformity to the foregoing principles or articles, and the acknowledged laws of the Nation.

Done in Legislative Council, at New Town, this 15th day of of[sic] June, 1825.

JNO. ROSS, Pres't N. Com.
MAJOR RIDGE
Speaker of Council,
his
Approved—PATH x KILLER,
mark
Principal Chief.

AMENDMENT TO THE INTER-MARRIAGE LAW.

New Town, Cherokee Nation, November 10th, 1825.

Resolved by the National Committee and Council, That the section embraced in the law regulating marriages between white men and Cherokee women and making it unlawful for white men to have more than one wife, and recommending all others, also, to have but one wife, be, and the same is, hereby amended, so that it shall not be lawful[sic] hereafter, for any person or persons, whatsoever, to have more than one wife.

JNO. ROSS, Pres't N. Com.
MAJOR RIDGE, Speaker
his
Approved—PATH x KILLER,
mark
CHAS. R. HICKS.

195

EARLY HISTORY OF CHEROKEES.

A. McCOY, Clerk N. Com.
E. BOUDINOTT, Clerk N. Council.

CONSTITUTIONAL DELEGATES ACT.

Whereas, the General Council of the Cherokee Nation, now in session, having taken into consideration the subject of adopting a Constitution for the future government of said Nation, and after mature deliberation, it is deemed expedient that a Convention be called and in order that the wishes of the people of the several Districts may be fairly represented on this all important subject.

It is hereby resolved by the National Committee and Council, That the persons hereinafter named be, and they are hereby nominated and recommended to the people of their respective Districts as candidates to run an election for seats in the Convention, and three out of the ten in each District who shall get the highest number of votes shall be elected, and for the convenience of the people in giving in their votes, three precincts in each District are selected and superintendents and clerks to the elections are chosen, and no person but a free male citizen who is full grown shall be entitled to vote for three of the candidates herein nominated in their respective Districts, and no vote by proxy shall be admitted, and that all the votes shall be given in viva voce, and in case of death, sickness or other incident which may occur to prevent all or any of the superintendents from attending at the several precincts to which they are chosen, the people of the respective precincts shall make a selection to fill such vacancies. And in case of similar incident occurring to any of the members elect, the person receiving the next highest number of votes shall supply the vacancy.

In Chickamauga District, John Ross, Richard Taylor, John Baldridge, Jas. Brown, Sleeping Rabbit, John Benge, Nathanial Hicks, Sicketowee, Jas. Starr and Daniel McCoy are nominated and recommended as candidates, and the election in the first precinct shall be held at or near Hicks' mill, and Charles R. Hicks and Archibald Fields are chosen superintendents, and Leonard Hicks, clerk. The election in the second precinct shall be held at or near Hunter Langley's in Lookout Valley, and James Lowrey and Robert Vann are chosen superintendents, and John Candy, clerk. The election in the third precinct shall be held at the courthouse, and Joseph Coodey and William S. Coodey are chosen

196

superintendents, and Robert Fields, clerk.

In Chattooga District, George Lowrey, Samuel Gunter, Andrew Ross, David Vann, David Brown, Spirit, The Bark, Salecooke, Edward Gunter and John Brown are nominated and recommended as candidates, and the election in the first precinct in this District shall be held at or near Edward Gunter's schoolhouse in Creek Path Valley, and Alexander Gilbreath and Dempsey Fields are chosen superintendents, and John Gunter, clerk. The election in the second precinct shall be held at or near Laugh at Mush's house, in Wills Valley, and William Chamberlin and Martin M'Intosh are chosen superintendents, and George Lowrey, Jr., clerk. The election in the third precinct shall be held at the courthouse, and Charles Vann and James M'Intosh are chosen superintendents, and Thomas Wilson, clerk.

In Coosewaytee District, John Martin, W. S. Adair, Elias Boudinott, Joseph Vann, John Ridge, William Hicks, Elijah Hicks, John Sanders, Kelechulah and Alex. McCoy are nominated and recommended as candidates. The election in the first precinct in this District shall be held at or near William Hicks' house on Coukillokee Creek, and Edward Adair and G. W. Adair are chosen superintendents, and Stand Watie, clerk. The election in the second precinct shall be held at Elechaye, and George Sanders and Robert Sanders are chosen superintendents, and James Sanders, clerk. The election in the third precinct shall be be[sic] held at the courthouse, and George Harlin and William Thompson are chosen superintendents, and Jos. M. Lynch, clerk.

In Ahmohee District, The Hair, Lewis Ross, Thos. Foreman, John Walker, Jr., Going Snake, George Fields, James Bigby, Deer-in-Water, John M'Intosh and Thomas Fields are nominated and recommended as candidates. The election in the first precinct in this District shall be held at or near Kalawee's house at Long Savannah, and Wm. Blythe and John Fields are chosen superintendents, and Ezekiel Fields, clerk. The election in the second precinct shall be held at or near Bridge Maker's house at Ahmohee Town, and Ezekiel Starr and Michael Hildebrand are chosen superintendents, and James McNair, clerk. The election in the third precinct shall be held at the courthouse, and David M'Nair and James M'Daniel are chosen superintendents, and T. W. Ross, clerk.

In Hickory Log District, James Daniel, George Still, Woman Killer, Robert Rogers, Moses Parris, John Duncan, Moses Downing,

George Ward, Tahquoh and Sam. Downing are nominated and recommended as candidates. The election in the first precinct in this District shall be held at or near George Welch's house, at the Cross Roads, and A. Hudson and E. Duncan are chosen superintendents, and Joshua Buffington, clerk. The election in the second precinct shall be held at or near Big Savannah, and John Downing and E. M'Laughlin are chosen superintendents, and John Daniel, clerk. The election in the third precinct shall be held at the courthouse, and John Wright and Ellis Harlin are chosen superintendents, and Moses Daniel, clerk.

In Hightower District, George M. Waters, Joseph Vann, Alexander Sanders, John Beamer, Walking Stick, Richard Rowe, The Feather, Old Field, Te-nah-la-wee-stah and Thomas Pettit are nominated and recommended as candidates. The election in the first precinct in this District shall be held at or near the Old Turkey's house, and Tahchi-see and John Harris are chosen superintendents, and Andrew Vann, clerk. The election in the second precinct shall be held at or near You-hah-lah-town house, and Kani-to-hee and Young Rogers are chosen superintendents, and John Sanders, clerk. The election in the third precinct shall be held at the courthouse, and Charles Moore and W. Thompson are chosen superintendents, and John Phillips, clerk.

In Aquohee District, Sitewake, Bald Town George, Richard Walker, John Timson, Allbone, Robin (Judge Walker's son-in-law), Ahtoheeskee, Kunsenee, Samuel Ward and Kalkalloskee are nominated and recommended as candidates. The election in the first precinct in this District shall be held at or near Tasquittee, and Thompson and Dick Downing are chosen superintendents, and William Reid, clerk. The election in the second precinct shall be held at or near Samuel Ward's house, and Isaac Tucker and John Bighead are chosen superintendents, and David England, clerk. The election at the third precinct shall be held at the courthouse, and Whirlwind and Bear Conjurer are chosen superintendent, and Rev. E. Jones, clerk.

Be it further resolved, That the election at the several places herein selected for each District shall be held on the Saturday previous to the commencement of the Courts for May term, next, and return of all the votes given shall be made to the superintendents of the election at the courthouse on the Monday following, being the first day of court, with a certificate of the polls, signed by the superintendents and clerks, and after all the votes being collected and rendered in, the three candidates having the highest number of votes shall be duly elected and the superintendents and clerks at the courthouse shall give to each of the members elected a certificate. And in case there shall be an equal number of votes between any of the three candidates, the members of the convention shall give them the casting vote, and that the superintendents shall, before entering upon their duties, take an oath for the faithful performance of their trusts, and that the members so elected shall, on the 4th day of July, next, meet at Echota and form a Convention and proceed to adopt a Constitution for the government of the Cherokee Nation.

Be it further resolved, That the principles which shall be established in the Constitution, to be adopted by the Convention, shall not in any degree go to destroy the rights and liberties of the free citizens of this Nation, nor to affect or impair the fundamental principles and laws, by which the Nation is now governed, and that the General Council to be convened in the fall of 1827 shall be held under the present existing authorities; Provided, nevertheless, that nothing shall be so construed on this last clause so as to invalidate or prevent the Constitution, adopted by the Convention, from going into effect after the foresaid next General Council.

JNO. ROSS, Pres't N. Com.

MAJOR RIDGE, Speaker.

his

Approved—PATH x KILLER,

mark

New Echota, October 13th, 1826.

ELIGIBILITY TO OFFICE.

New Echota, Cherokee Nation, October 13th, 1826.

Resolved by the National Committee and Council, That no person who disbelieves in the existence of the Creator, and or rewards and punishments after death, shall be eligible to hold any office under the government of the Cherokee Nation, nor be allowed the privilege of his or her testimony in any court of justice.

JNO. ROSS, Pres't N. Com.

MAJOR RIDGE, Speaker

his

Approved—PATH x KILLER,

mark

199

A. McCOY, Clerk N. Com.
E. BOUDINOTT, Clerk N. Council.

CONSTITUTION

of

THE CHEROKEE NATION:

Formed by a Convention of Delegates

From the Several Districts

AT NEW ECHOTA,

July, 1827

   We, the Representatives of the people of the Cherokee Nation, in Convention assembled, in order to establish justice, ensure tranquility, promote our common welfare and secure to ourselves and our posterity the blessings of liberty; acknowledging with humility and gratitude the goodness of the sovereign Ruler of the Universe, in offering us an opportunity so favorable to the design, and imploring His aid and direction in its accomplishment, do ordain and establish this Constitution for the Government of the Cherokee Nation.
   Article 1. Sec. 1. The boundaries of this Nation, embracing the lands solemnly guaranteed and reserved forever to the Cherokee Nation by the treaties concluded with the United States, are as follows, and shall forever hereafter remain unalterably the same, to wit:
   Beginning on the north bank of the Tennessee River at the upper part of the Chickasaw old field, thence along the main channel of said river, including all the islands therein, to the mouth of the Hiwassee River, thence up the main channel of said river, including all islands, to the first hill which closes in on said river about two miles above Hiwassee Old Town, thence along the ridge which divides the waters of the Hiwassee and Little Tillico, to the Tennessee River at Tallassee, thence along the main channel, including islands, to the junction of the Cowee and Nanteyalee, thence along the ridge in the fork of said river, to the top of the blue ridge, thence along the blue ridge to the Unicoy Turnpike road, thence by a straight line to the main source of the

200

Chestatee, thence along its main channel, including islands, to the Chattahoochy, and thence down the same to the Creek boundary at Buzzard Roost, thence along the boundary line which separates this and the Creek Nation, to a point on the Coosa River opposite the mouth of Wills Creek, thence down along the south bank of the same to a point opposite to Fort Strother, thence up the river to the mouth of Wills Creek, thence up along the east bank of said creek to the west branch thereof, and up the same to its source, and thence along the ridge which separates the Tombeccee and Tennessee waters to a point on the top of said ridge, thence due north to Camp Coffee on Tennessee River, which is opposite the Chickasaw Island, thence to the place of beginning.

Sec. 2. The sovereignty and Jurisdiction of this Government shall extend over the country within the boundaries above described, and the lands therein are, and shall remain, the common property of the Nation, but the improvements made thereon, and in the possession of the citizens of the Nation, are the exclusive and indefeasible property of the citizens respectively who made, or may rightfully be in possession of them; Provided, that the citizens of the Nation, possessing exclusive and indefeasible right to their respective improvements, as expressed in this article, shall possess no right nor power to dispose of their improvements in any manner whatever to the United States, individual states nor individual citizens thereof, and that whenever any such citizen or citizens shall remove with their effects out of the limits of this Nation, and become citizens of any other government, all their rights and privileges as citizens of this Nation shall cease; Provided, nevertheless, that the Legislature shall have power to readmit by law to all the rights of citizenship any such person or persons who may at any time desire to return to the Nation on their memorializing the General Council for such readmission. Moreover, the Legislature shall have power to adopt such laws and regulations, as its wisdom may deem expedient and proper, to prevent the citizens from monopolizing improvements with the view of speculation.

Article II. Sec. 1. The power of this Government shall be divided into three distinct departments: The Legislative, the Executive and Judicial.

Sec. 2. No person or persons belonging to one of these Departments shall exercise any of the powers properly belonging to either of the others, except in the cases hereinafter expressly directed or permitted.

Article III. Sec. 1. The Legislative power shall be vested in two distinct branches: a Committee and a Council, each to have a negative on the other, and both to be styled the General Council of the Cherokee Nation, and the style of their acts and laws shall be:

"RESOLVED by the Committee and Council, in General Council convened."

Sec. 2. The Cherokee Nation, as laid off into eight Districts, shall so remain.

Sec. 3. The Committee shall consist of two members from each District, and the Council shall consist of three members from each District, to be chosen by the qualified electors of their respective Districts, for two years, and the elections to be held in every District on the first Monday in August, for the year 1828, and every succeeding two years thereafter, and the General Council shall be held once a year, to be convened on the second Monday of October in each year, at New Echota.

Sec. 4. No person shall be eligible to a seat in the General Council but a free Cherokee Male Citizen, who shall have attained the age of twenty-five years. The descendants of Cherokee men by all free women, except the African race, whose parents may have been living together as man and wife, according to the customs and laws of this Nation, shall be entitled to all the rights and privileges of this Nation, as well as the posterity of Cherokee women by all free men. No person who is of negro or mulatto parentage, either by the father or mother side, shall be eligible to hold any office of profit, honor or trust under this Government.

Sec. 5. The electors and members of the General Council shall, in all cases except those of treason, felony or breach of peace, be privileged from arrest during their attendance at election, and at the General Council, and in going to and returning from the same.

Sec. 6. In all elections by the people, the electors shall vote viva voce. Electors for members to the General Council for 1828 shall be held at the places of holding the several courts, and at the other two precincts in each District which are designated by the law under which the members of this Convention were elected, and the District Judges shall superintend the elections within the precincts of their respective Courthouses, and the Marshals and Sheriffs shall superintend within the

Robert L. Owen. Cherokee genealogy No. XIII—$1^1 4^2 2^3$. Ex-Secretary of the Cherokee National Board of Education and present (1916) United States Senator from Oklahoma.

precincts which may be assigned them by the Circuit Judges, who shall also appoint a clerk to each precinct. The superintendents and clerks shall, on the Wednesday morning succeeding the election, assemble at their respective Courthouses and proceed to examine and ascertain the true state of the polls, and shall issue to each member, duly elected, a certificate, and also make an official return of the state of the polls of the election to the Principal Chief, and it shall be the duty of the Sheriffs to deliver the same to the Executive; Provided, nevertheless, the General Council shall have power after the election of 1828 to regulate by law the precincts and superintendents and clerks of elections in the several Districts.

Sec. 7. All free male citizens (excepting negroes and descendants of white and Indian men by negro women who may have been set free), who shall have attained to the age of eighteen years, shall be equally entitled to vote at all public elections.

Sec. 8. Each house of the General Council shall judge of the qualifications and returns of its own members.

Sec. 9. Each house of the General Council may determine the rules of its proceedings, punish a member for disorderly behavior, and, with the concurrence of two-thirds, expel a member, but not a second time for the same cause.

Sec. 10. Each house of the General Council, when assembled, shall choose its own officers; a majority of each house shall constitute a quorum to do business, but a smaller number may adjourn from day to day and compel the attendance of absent members in such manner and under such penalty as each house may prescribe.

Sec. 11. The members of the Committee shall each receive from the Public Treasury a compensation for their services, which shall be two dollars and fifty cents per day during their attendance at the General Council, and the members of the Council shall each receive two dollars per day for their services during their attendance at the General Council: Provided, That the same may be increased or diminished by law, but no alteration shall take effect during the period of service of the members of the General Council, by whom such alteration shall have been made.

Sec. 12. The General Council shall regulate by law by whom and in what manner writs of elections shall be issued to fill the vacancies which may happen in either branch thereof.

Sec. 13. Each member of the General Council, before he takes his seat, shall take the following oath or affirmation, to wit:

"I. A. B., do solemnly swear (of affirm, as the case may be), that I have not obtained my election by bribery, or threats or any undue and unlawful means used by myself, or others by my desire or approbation, for that purpose; that I consider myself constitutionally qualified as a member of, and that, on all questions and measures which may come before me, I will so give my vote, and so conduct myself, as may in my judgment appear most conducive to the interest and prosperity of this Nation; and that I will bear the true faith and allegiance to the same, and to the utmost of my ability and power, observe, conform to, support and defend the Constitution thereof."

Sec. 14. No person who maybe convicted of felony before any court of this Nation shall be eligible to any office or appointment of honor, profit or trust within this Nation.

Sec. 15. The General Council shall have power to make all laws and regulations which they shall deem necessary and proper for the good of the Nation, which shall not be contrary to this Constitution.

Sec. 16. It shall be the duty of the General Council to pass such laws as may be necessary and proper, to decide differences by arbitrators to be appointed by the parties, who may choose that summary mode of adjustment.

Sec. 17. No power of suspending the laws of this Nation shall be exercised, unless by the Legislature of its authority.

Sec. 18. No retrospective law, nor any law impairing the obligations of contracts shall be passed.

Sec. 19. The Legislature shall have power to make laws for laying and collecting taxes for the purpose of raising a revenue.

Sec. 20. All bills making appropriations shall originate in the Committee, but the Council may propose amendments or reject the same.

Sec. 21. All other bills may originate in either house, subject to the concurrence or rejection of the other.

Sec. 22. All acknowledged treaties shall be the supreme law of the land.

Sec. 23. The General Council shall have the sole power of deciding on the construction of all treaty stipulations.

Sec. 24. The Council shall have the sole power of impeaching.

Sec. 25. All impeachments shall be tried by the Committee; when sitting for that purpose, the members shall be upon oath or affirmation; and no person shall be convicted without the concurrence of two-thirds of the members present.

Sec. 26. The Principal Chief, Assistant Principal Chief and all civil officers, under this Nation, shall be liable to impeachment for any misdemeanor in office, but judgment, in such cases, shall not extend further than removal from office and disqualification to hold any office of honor, trust or profit under this Nation. The party, whether convicted or acquitted, shall, nevertheless, be liable to indictment, trial, judgment and punishment according to law.

Article IV. Sec. 1. The supreme executive power of this Nation shall be vested in the Principal Chief, who shall be chosen by the General Council, and shall hold his office four years, to be elected as follows: The General Council, by a joint vote, shall be their second annual session after the rising of this Convention, and at every fourth annual session thereafter, on the second day after the Houses shall be organized and competent to proceed to business, elect a Principal Chief.

Sec. 2. No person, except a natural born citizen, shall be eligible to the office of Principal Chief, neither shall any person be eligible to that office who shall not have attained to the age of thirty-five years.

Sec. 3. There shall also be chosen at the same time by the General Council, in the same manner for four years, an Assistant Principal Chief.

Sec. 4. In case of the removal of the Principal Chief from office, or of his death, resignation or inability to discharge the powers and duties of the said office, the same shall devolve on the Assistant Principal Chief, until the inability be removed or the vacancy filled by the General Council.

Sec. 5. The General Council may, by law, provide for the case of removal, death, resignation or inability of both the Principal and Assistant Principal Chiefs, declaring what officer shall then act as Principal Chief until the disability be removed or a Principal Chief shall be elected.

Sec. 6. The Principal Chief shall, at stated times, receive for their services a compensation which shall neither be increased nor diminished during the period for which they shall have been elected, and they shall not receive, within that period, any other employment from the Cherokee Nation or any other government.

Sec. 7. Before the Principal Chief enters on the execution of his office he shall take the following oath, or affirmation: "I do solemnly swear (or affirm) that I will faithfully execute the office of Principal Chief of the Cherokee Nation and will, to the best of my ability, preserve, protect and defend the Constitution of the Cherokee Nation."

Sec. 8. He may, on extraordinary occasions, convene the General Council at the seat of government.

Sec. 9. He shall from time to time give to the General Council information of the state of the government and recommend to their consideration such measures as he may think expedient.

Sec. 10. He shall take care that the laws be faithfully executed.

Sec. 11. It shall be his duty to visit the different Districts at least once in two years to inform himself of the general condition of the Country.

Sec. 12. The Assistant Principal Chief shall, by virtue of his office, aid and advise the Principal Chief in the administration of the Government at all times during his continuance in office.

Sec. 13. Vacancies that may happen in offices, the appointment of which is vested in the General Council, shall be filled by the Principal Chief, during the recess of the General Council, by granting commissions which shall expire at the end of the next session.

Sec, 14. Every bill which shall have passed both Houses of the General Council, shall before it becomes a law, be presented to the Principal Chief of the Cherokee Nation. If he approve[sic], he shall sign it, but if not, he shall return it, with his objections, to the House in which it shall have originated, who shall enter the objections at large on their journals, and proceed to reconsider it. If, after such reconsideration, two-thirds of that House shall agree to pass the bill, it shall be sent, together with the objections, to the other House, by which it shall likewise be reconsidered, and if approved by two-thirds of that House, it shall become a law. If any bill shall not be returned by the Principal Chief within five days (Sundays excepted) after it shall have been presented to him, the same shall be a law, in like manner as if he had signed it, unless the General Council, by their adjournment, prevent its return, in which case it shall be a law, unless sent back within three days after their next meeting.

Sec. 15. Members of the General Council and all officers, Executive and Judicial, shall be bound by oath to support the Constitution of this Nation, and to perform the duties of their respective offices with fidelity.

Sec. 16. In case of disagreement between the two houses with respect to the time of adjournment, the Principal Chief shall have power to adjourn the General Council to such a time as he thinks proper, provided it be not a period beyond the next constitutional meeting of the same.

Sec. 17. The Principal Chief shall, during the sitting of the General Council, attend to the seat of government.

Sec. 18. There shall be a Council to consist of three men, to be appointed by the joint vote of both Houses, to advise the Principal Chief in the Executive part of the Government, over whom the Principal Chief shall have full power, at his discretion, to assemble, and he, together with the Assistant Principal Chief and the Counsellors[sic] or a majority of them, may, from time to time, hold and keep a Council for ordering and directing the affairs of the Nation according of law.

Sec. 19. The members of the council shall be chosen for the term of one year.

Sec. 20. The resolutions and advice of the Council shall be recorded in a register and signed by the members agreeing therto[sic], which may be called for by either House of the General Council, and any counsellor[sic] may enter his dissent to the resolution of the majority.

Sec. 21. The Treasurer of the Cherokee Nation shall be chosen by the joint vote of both Houses of the General Council for the term of two years.

Sec. 22. The Treasurer shall, before entering on the duties of his officer, give bond to the Nation, with sureties to the satisfaction of the Legislature, for the faithful discharge of his trust.

Sec. 23. No money shall be drawn from the Treasury but by warrant from the Principal Chief, and in consequence of appropriations made by law.

Sec. 24. It shall be the duty of the Treasurer to receive all public monies and to make a regular statement and account of the receipts and expenditures of all public monies at the annual session of the General Council.

Article V. Sec. 1. The judicial powers shall be vested in a Supreme Court, and such Circuit and Inferior Courts as the General Council may from time to time ordain and establish.

Sec. 2. The Supreme Court shall consist of three judges, any two of whom shall be a quorum.

Sec. 3. The judges of each shall hold their commissions four years, but any of them may be removed from office on the address of two-thirds of each House of the General Council to the Principal Chief for that purpose.

Sec. 4. The judges of the Supreme and Circuit courts shall, at stated times, receive a compensation, which shall not be diminished during their continuance in office, but they shall receive no fees or perquisites of office, nor hold any other office of profit or any other power.

Sec. 5, No person shall be appointed a judge of any of the courts before he shall have attained to the age of thirty years, nor shall any person continue to execute the duties of any of the said offices after he shall have attained to the age of seventy years.

Sec. 6. The judges of the Supreme and Circuit courts shall be appointed by a joint vote of both Houses of the General Council.

Sec. 7. There shall be appointed in each District, under the Legislative authority, as many Justices of the Peace as it may be deemed the public good requires, whose powers, duties and duration of office shall be clearly designated.

Sec. 8 The judges of the Supreme Court and Circuit Courts shall have complete criminal jurisdiction in such cases and in such manner as may be pointed out by law.

Sec. 9. Each Court shall choose its own clerks for the term of four years, but such clerks shall not continue in office unless their qualifications shall be adjudged and approved by the judges of the Superior Court and they shall be removable for breach of good behavior at any time by the judges of their respective courts.

Sec. 10. No judge shall sit on trial of any cause where the parties shall be connected with him by affinity or consanguinity, except by consent of the parties. In case all the judges of the Supreme Court shall be interested in the event of any cause, or related to all or either of the parties, the Legislature may provide by law for the selection of three men of good character and knowledge for the determination thereof, who shall be especially commissioned by the Principal Chief for the case.

Sec. 11. All writs and other process shall run in the name of the Cherokee Nation, and bear test and be signed by the respective clerks.

Sec. 12. Indictments shall conclude, "against the peace and

dignity of the Cherokee Nation."

Sec. 13. The Supreme Court shall hold its sessions annually at the seat of government, to be convened on the second Monday of October in each year.

Sec. 14. In all criminal prosecutions, the accused shall have the right of being heard, of demanding the nature and cause of the accusation against him, of meeting the witnesses face to face, of having compulsory process for obtaining witnesses in his favor, and in prosecutions by indictment or information, a speedy public trial by an impartal[sic] jury of the vicinage, nor shall he be compelled to give evidence against himself.

Sec. 15. The people shall be secure in their persons, houses, papers and possessions from unreasonable seizures and searches, and no warrant to search any place or to seize any person or things shall be issued without describing them as nearly as may be, nor without good cause, supported by oath or affirmation. All prisoners shall be bailable by sufficient securities, unless of capital offenses, where the proof is evident or presumption great.

Article VI. Sec. 1. Whereas, the ministers of the Gospel are by their profession dedicated to the service of God and the care of souls and ought not to be diverted from the great duty of their function, therefore, no minister of the Gospel or public preacher of any religious persuasion, whilst he continues in the exercise of his pastoral functions, shall be eligible to the office of Principal Chief, or a seat in either House of the General Council.

Sec. 2. No person who denies the being of a God, or a future state of rewards and punishment, shall hold any office in the civil department of this Nation.

Sec. 3. The free exercise of religious worship and serving God without distinction shall forever be allowed within this Nation; Provided, That this liberty of conscience shall not be so construed as to excuse acts of licentiousness or justify practices inconsistent with the peace or safety of this Nation.

Sec. 4. Whenever the General Council shall determine the expediency of appointing delegates or other public agents for the purpose of transacting business with the government of the United States, the power to recommend, and by the advice and consent of the committee, shall appoint and commission such delegates or public agents accordingly, and all matters of interest touching the rights of the citizens of this Nation which may require the attention of the government of the United States, the Principal Chief shall keep up a friendly correspondence with that government, through the medium of its proper officers.

Sec. 5. All commissions shall be in the name and by the authority of the Cherokee Nation, and be sealed with the seal of the Nation and signed by the Principal Chief.

The Principal Chief shall make use of his private seal until a National seal shall be provided.

Sec. 6. A sheriff shall be elected in each District by the qualified electors thereof, who shall hold his office for the term of two years, unless sooner removed. Should a vacancy occur subsequent to an election, it shall be filled by the Principal Chief, as in other cases, and the person so appointed shall continue in office until the next general election, when such vacancy shall be filled by the qualified electors, and the sheriff then elected shall continue in office for two years.

Sec. 7. There shall be a marshall[sic] appointed by a joint vote of both Houses of the General Council, for the term of four years, whose compensation and duties shall be regulated by law, and whose jurisdiction shall extend over the Cherokee Nation.

Sec. 8. No person shall for the same offense be twice put in jeopary[sic] of life or limb, nor shall any person's property be taken or applied to public use without his consent: Provided, That nothing in this clause shall be so construed as to impair the right and power of the General Council to lay and collect taxes. All courts shall be open and every person for an injury done him, in his property, person or reputation, shall have remedy by due course of law.

Sec. 9. The right of trial by jury shall remain inviolate.

Sec. 10. Religion, morality and knowledge being necessary to good government, the preservation of liberty and the happiness of mankind, schools and the means of education shall forever be encouraged in this Nation.

Sec. 11. The appointment of all officers not otherwise directed by this Constitution, shall be vested in the Legislature.

Sec. 12. All Laws in force in this Nation at the passing of this Constitution shall so continue until altered or repealed by the Legislature, except where they are temporary, in which case they shall expire at the times respectively limited for their duration, if not continued by an act of the Legislature.

Sec. 13. The General Council may at any time propose such amendments to this Constitution as two-thirds of each House shall deem expedient, and the Principal Chief shall issue a proclamation directing all the civil officers of the several Districts to promulgate the same as extensively as possible within their respective Districts, at least nine months previous to the next general election, and, if at the first session of the General Council after such general election, two-thirds of each House shall, by yeas and nays, ratify such proposed amendments, they shall be valid to all intents and purposes as parts of this Constitution: Provided, That such proposed amendments shall be read on three several days in each House, as well as when the same are proposed as when they are ratified.

Done in Convention at New Echota, this twenty-sixth day of July, in the year of our Lord, one thousand eight hundred and twenty-seven. In testimony whereof, we have each of us, hereunto subscribed our names.

JNO. ROSS, Pres't N. Com.

Jno. Baldridge, Geo. Lowrey, Jno. Brown, Edward Gunter, John Martin, Joseph Vann, Kelechulee, Lewis Ross, Thomas Foreman, Hair Conrad, James Daniel, John Duncan, Joseph Vann, Thomas Petitt, John Beamer, Ooclenota, Wm. Boling, John Timson, Situwakee, Richard Walker.

A. McCOY, Sec'y to Com.

AN EDUCATIONAL ACT.

Resolved by the Committee and Council, in General Council Convened, That there shall be appointed by the Principal Chief of the Cherokee Nation two committees of two members each, one in each judicial circuit, whose duty it shall be to visit the different schools in the Nation, within the respective Districts of their circuits, at the public examinations of said schools, once a year, and to report to the General Council annually on the number of scholars, progress of education, etc.

Be it Further Resolved, That they shall be paid one dollar a day, while in actual service, out of any monies in the National Treasury not otherwise appropriated.

LEWIS ROSS, Pres't Com.
Concurred— GOING SNAKE, Speaker,
Approved Nov. 6th—JNO. ROSS,
New Echota, October 30th, 1828.

DISTURBANCE OF DIVINE WORSHIP.

Resolved by the Committee and Council, in General Council Convened, That, if any person or persons shall interrupt, by misbehavior, any congregation of Cherokee or white citizens, assembled at any place for the purpose of Divine worship, such person or persons so offending shall, upon conviction thereof before any of the courts, be fined in a sum not exceeding ten dollars, to be adjudged by the court of the District in which such offense may be committed, and if any negro slave shall be convicted of the above offense he shall be punished with thirty-nine stripes on the bare back.

LEWIS ROSS, Pres't N. Com
Approved— JNO. ROSS.
New Echota, November 12th, 1828.

SALARIES ACT.

Resolved by the Committee and Council, in General Council Convened, That, the Principal Chief of the Cherokee Nation shall be allowed a salary of three hundred dollars per annum, during his continuance in office, out of the public funds of the Nation. And the Assistant Principal Chief shall be allowed a salary of one hundred and fifty dollars.

The Executive Counsellors[sic] shall be paid at the rate of two dollars per day, while in actual service, when called upon by the Principal Chief.

The Treasurer of the Cherokee Nation shall be allowed for his services three hundred and fifty dollars per annum.

The sheriffs of the several Districts shall be allowed for their services fifty dollars per annum, besides their collection fees—any law to the contrary notwithstanding.

LEWIS ROSS, Pres't Com.
Concurred— GOING SNAKE, Speaker Coun.
Approved— JNO. ROSS.
New Echota, November 13th, 1828.

ELECTION PRECINCTS CREATED.

Resolved by the Committee and Council, in General Council Convened, That, the elections to be holden[sic] hereafter in the several Districts for members of the General Council, sheriffs and constables, shalls[sic] be held at the following precincts until otherwise altered by the General Council, viz: Chickamuaga District: The first precinct to be at the court house, the second at Hunter Langly's, in Lookout Valley; third at Hicks' Mill, and the fourth at Kah-Noh-Cloo's. Chatooga District: First precinct at the court house; second at Ah-ne-lah-ka-yah's, in Turkey Tows[sic]; Third at James Field's, Turnip Mountain; fourth at Laugh-at-mush's, Will's Valley; fifth at Edward Gunter's, in Creek Path, and sixth at Raccoon Town, at Little Turtle's house. Coosewatee District: First at the court house, and the third at Ellijay. Ahmohee District: First at the court house; second at Squires, in Long Savannah; third at Chee-squah-ne-ta's; fourth at Swimmers, Highwassee Old Town. Hickory Log District: First at the court house; second at the old court house; third at or near Big Savannah. Hightower District: First at the court house; second at Pipe's Spring; third at Yon-hah-house; second at Choowalookee's; third at Oowatee's; fourth at Skenah Town; fifth at Beach Town. Aquohee District: First at the court house; second at Lame Dick's; third at Highwassee Town; fourth at widow Nettle Carriers'; fifth at Chee-yoh-ee.

Be it Further Resolved, That, two superintendents and one clerk shall be appointed to take the votes at each precinct, and it shall be the duty of the circuit judges respectively to make such appointments while on their judicial circuit last preceeding[sic] the general elections for members of the General Council, and shall notify the managers and clerks of their appointment, by the sheriff of the District, and in case wither of the circuit judges fail to hold his courts agreeably to law, or any of the managers or clerks shall refuse to act, the District judge shall be authorized to fill such vacancies, and in case any shall fail to attend on the day of the election the voters shall be allowed to choose some suitable person or persons to act in his or their stead.

Be it Further Resolved, That, the clerks shall particularly take down the names of all persons voting and for whom they may vote, and the managers and clerks shall meet at the court house in their respective Districts on the Wednesday succeeding the election, then and there to count the votes and issue a certificate to each member elect of his constitutional election.

Be it Further Resolved, That, the managers and clerks while acting shall be upon oath and shall not be entitled to receive any compensation from the National Treasury for their services.

Approved—JNO. ROSS.

New Echota, November 2d, 1829.

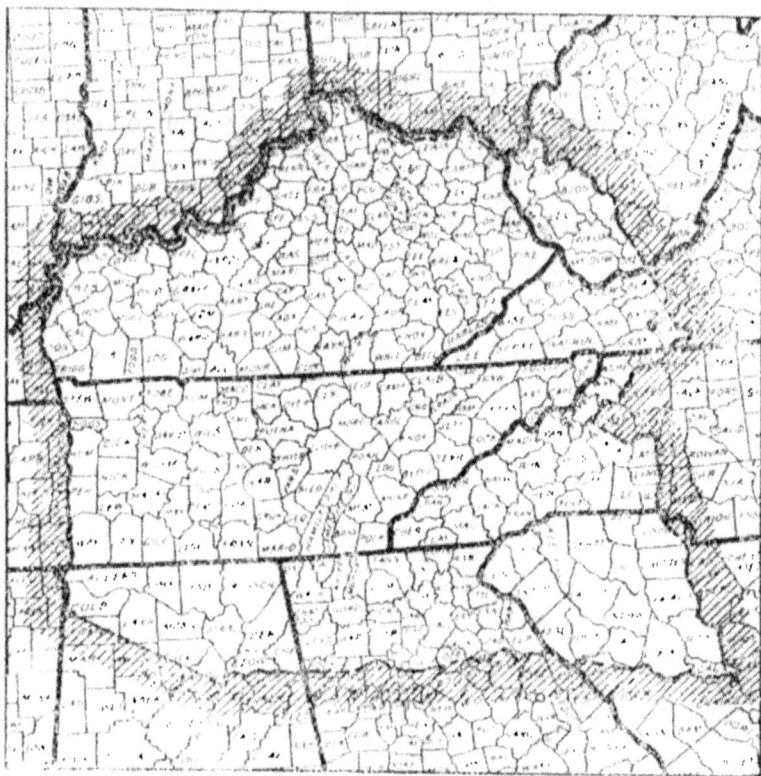

Map of Cherokee Territory in 1720.

Subject Index

Subject Index

www.ingramcontent.com/pod-product-compliance
Lightning Source LLC
Chambersburg PA
CBHW070405270326

41926CB00014B/2711